"Strausbaugh, a masterful explorer of New York's vivid past, turns his keen eye now on how the city's art and culture were transformed by Marcel Duchamp. Strausbaugh reminds us not only of Duchamp's triumphs, but also what American artists have derived from his provocative and monumental mischief." —Richard Byrne, author of *Hotel Mayflower* and *Beauty Doesn't Reach Me*

"Defines the man and the moment that pushed the art world beyond 'the tyranny of good taste' and helped it find true power." —Ilise S. Carter, author of *When We Talked to the Dead: How Ghosts Gave American Women Their Voice*

•

Artist, anti-artist, joker, trickster, shape-shifter: Marcel Duchamp broke with tradition and pushed the avant-garde decisively forward. When his work exploded like an art bomb in New York in the 1910s, American art was still mired in the nineteenth century. Duchamp, bored with tradition, reimagined what art could be, what it was for, and how it might be made—hanging a snow shovel from the ceiling, inverting a urinal, "painting" with dust and bits of string between panes of glass, and reducing his entire oeuvre into a briefcase of miniatures. *Duchamp Takes New York* traces this bold, playful energy,

showing how the city inspired and staged his avant-garde experiments.

Duchamp's offhand gestures reshaped the course of twentieth-century American art, laying the groundwork for nearly every major movement that followed. And then, at the height of his influence, Duchamp appeared to walk away—declaring himself finished with art and devoting his energies to becoming a chess champion instead. Only after his death did it emerge that he had spent two decades secretly working on one final, unsettling work, leaving the world to try to comprehend it without explanation—his ultimate prank.

John Strausbaugh, a longtime chronicler of the city, puts New York at the center of Duchamp's story. Fleeing the comforts of French bourgeois life—"wives, three children, a country house, three cars!"—Duchamp found New York instantly liberating. It was here that he produced much of his most radical work and eventually settled for good, once declaring, "New York itself is a complete work of art." Duchamp's art simply can't be pinned down, without first recognizing his relationship to New York.

Duchamp Takes New York
Duchamp Takes New York
Duchamp Takes New York
Duchamp Takes New York
Duchamp Takes New York
Duchamp Takes New York

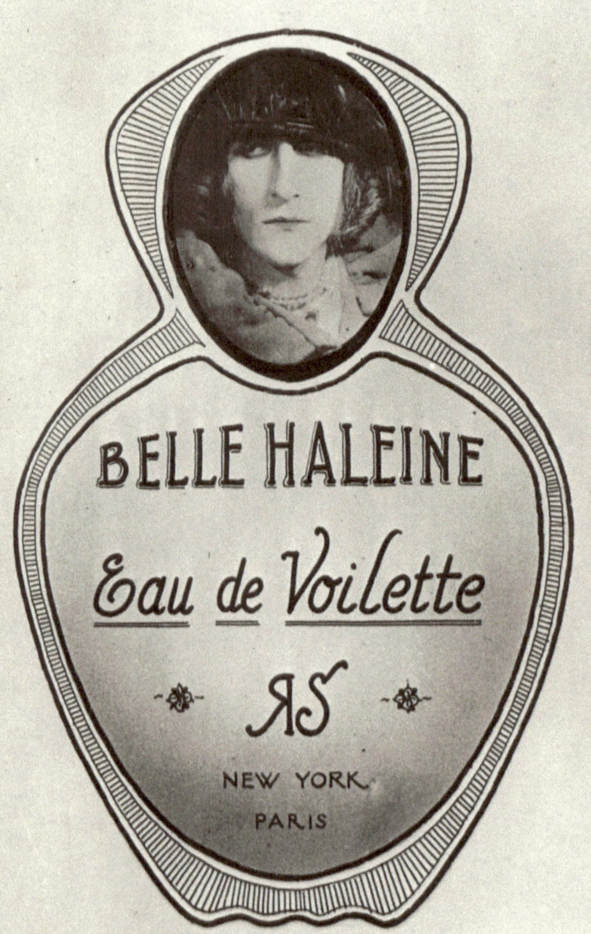

BELLE HALEINE
Eau de Voilette
RS
NEW YORK.
PARIS

Duchamp Takes New York

John Strausbaugh

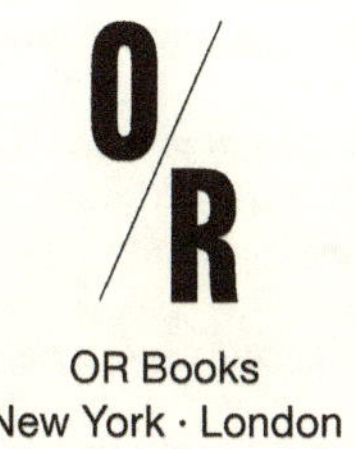

OR Books
New York · London

Published by OR Books, New York and London

Visit our website at www.orbooks.com

All rights information: rights@orbooks.com

First printing 2026

The manufacturer's authorised representative in the EU for product safety is Authorised Rep Compliance Ltd, 71 Lower Baggot Street, Dublin D02 P593 Ireland (www.arccompliance.com)

paperback ISBN 978-1-68219-457-7 · ebook ISBN 978-1-68219-458-4

Cover: Five-Way Portrait of Marcel Duchamp, taken at the Broadway Photo Shop, Broadway and 48th Street, New York, NY, June 21, 1917. Digital image © CNAC/MNAM, Dist. RMN-Grand Palais / Art Resource, NY

Frontispiece: "Belle Haleine: Eau de Voilette (Nice Breath: Veil Water)." The label is a part of a photograph published on the cover of *New York Dada*, New York, April 1921. Wikimedia Commons

page 155: Jean Crotti, 1915, *Portrait of Marcel Duchamp* (Sculpture made to measure), mixed media. Exhibited Montross Gallery 4–22 April 1916, New York City. Sculpture lost or destroyed. Wikimedia Commons

Cover and book design and typesetting by Laura Lindgren

Duchamp Takes New York

1 The *Nude* Descends on New York City

It was a good show, but don't do it again.

On February 17, 1913, the International Exhibition of Modern Art opened in New York City with great fanfare. It ran for a tumultuous month. Because it was housed in the 69th Regiment Armory, a barrel-vaulted hall that still looms over Lexington Avenue at 25th Street, it came to be known simply as the Armory Show. It was the first time Americans, outside a tiny handful of art cognoscenti, saw works by Pablo Picasso, Vincent van Gogh, Paul Gauguin, Georges Seurat, Georges Rouault, Henri Matisse, Georges Braque, Edvard Munch, Fernand Léger, Odilon Redon, Constantin Brâncuşi, Paul Cézanne, Honoré Daumier, Francis Picabia, Wassily Kandinsky . . . an astounding explosion of modern art. Fauvists, Impressionists, Post-Impressionists, Cubists, all thrown together in one giant show, all previously unseen in the

United States. Americans would never look at art or make art the same way again.

At the center of this whirlwind of shocking new art was one painting that was singled out again and again as representing everything that was different, startling, and just plain weird about it all: *Nude Descending a Staircase, No. 2*, by a twenty-five-year-old Frenchman nobody had heard of before, Marcel Duchamp. Who at the time was in Paris, completely unaware of the stir his painting was causing across the Atlantic. He was studying to become a librarian.

The exhibition was such a sensation because American visual art in 1913 was stuck somewhere back in the nineteenth century, if not the Renaissance. It had never been encouraged to develop. Americans devoured writing, music, and theater, but they had not warmed to painting and sculpture. Every small town had its piano teacher, but very few had an art teacher. After the Civil War, art was increasingly segmented into highbrow and lowbrow, an esthetic divide along class lines. Lowbrow meant the pop culture that entertained the lower and lower-middle classes—minstrel shows, vaudeville, Currier & Ives, the nickelodeon. Fine art was reserved for those with the education, esthetic refinement, and taste to appreciate it correctly, which restricted its appeal to small circles of wealthy patrons and cognoscenti in New York and a few other cities.

Even in those refined circles, art, like all endeavors in the land of the Protestant work ethic, was supposed to serve some pragmatic purpose. "For Americans an artist had always been valued for his functional role," art historian Dore Ashton noted. Artists were thought to be not terribly different from artisans and craftsmen; a well-painted landscape was the functional equivalent of a well-constructed chair. Also, American painters and sculptors were still struggling to find an authentically American style, long after American literature and music (at least popular music) had established themselves. It did not help that American educators, curators, and critics saw their role as preserving old forms and hallowed traditions against change. As of 1913, American sculpture was still largely neoclassical. Paintings were still mostly traditionally rendered portraits, landscapes, or historical scenes (preferably American subjects, scenes, and history). About the most avant-garde American painting got in 1913 was the New York Realists school, painters such as John Sloan and George Bellows who used traditional methods but painted scenes of city life—a prizefight, wash hung from a line between tenements—generally considered to be beneath the purview of fine art. They were nicknamed the Ashcan School, originally an insult, but it stuck.

Those few Americans who did want to see modern art had two choices. They could travel to Paris, tour the museums and galleries and studios, if possible meet the expats Leo Stein and his sister Gertrude, who had moved to Paris in 1903 and knew more about the European avant-garde than any other Americans then living. Or they could visit Alfred Stieglitz's Little Galleries of the Photo-Secession, a small space at 291 Fifth Avenue. In 1905 Hoboken-born Stieglitz originally opened "291," as it was commonly known, with the mission of proving that photography could be fine art—a notion met with skepticism in a land where photography meant tintype family portraits. It wasn't such a great leap when Stieglitz began showing new paintings, drawings, and sculpture as well. Before the Armory Show, 291 had already introduced a very small core of New York art connoisseurs to work by Picasso, Auguste Rodin, Matisse, and Cézanne.

In the 1910s the dominant art institution in New York, the National Academy of Design, was a staunchly conservative defender of the old forms and a bitter enemy of the new. As early as 1875 disaffected artists had broken off to form the Art Students League on West 57th Street. Pointedly opposed to the National Academy's closed and elitist system of conferring favor on a handful of approved artists, the Art Students League was an open atelier where anyone could study with any teacher they chose. In 1911 they formed the Association of American Painters and Sculptors (AAPS). It was the AAPS, determined to drag the American art world into the new century, who organized the Armory Show.

"The exhibition," art historian Milton Brown wrote, "had been calculated from the beginning as a mental jolt to stir America out of its long esthetic complacency." Two of the organizing artists, Walt Kuhn and Arthur B. Davies, sailed to Paris, then the undisputed capital of Western art, looking for new work for the show. They met resident American artist Walter Pach, who took them to see Picabia, Redon, and Brâncuşi; and to meet Leo and Gertrude Stein, through whom they saw the work of the two leading Cubists, Picasso and Braque; and Pach showed them works by Duchamp and his brothers. Davies called Duchamp's work "the strongest expression I've seen yet!" Kuhn and Davies crated four of his paintings and shipped them to New York.

Duchamp did not meet with them.

•

Henri-Robert-Marcel Duchamp, born in 1887, grew up in a comfortable, bourgeois household in Blainville, Normandy. His father was a notary, a well-paid and respected position in those days, and for a decade served as the mayor of Blainville. Marcel grew up surrounded by art. His maternal grandfather was a well-known painter and engraver. Both of his older brothers, Gaston and Raymond, who signed their work Jacques Villon and Raymond Duchamp-Villon, were artists, as was his sister Suzanne. Their father, a good dad, supported them with modest stipends.

Marcel was painting by the age of fifteen. He diligently worked his way through the modern movements of the day—Fauvism, Impressionism, Cubism. In 1909, when he turned twenty-two, his brothers started hosting Sunday gatherings of mostly Cubist artists but also writers; among them were Picabia and Guillaume Apollinaire. The three remained friends through the turbulent years to come.

In 1909 Duchamp's work was in a few group shows, but it wasn't until 1912 that he discovered his own recognizable style. In January of that year he produced the painting that would make him famous and infamous: *Nude Descending a Staircase, No. 2.* The figure in it is not discernibly human. It looks mechanical, like a shiny bronze robot. It appears to be tumbling down the stairs as in a blizzard of film stills. (Duchamp rejected any allusions to cinema, but it fits.) In depicting the figure moving in fragments, he was inspired by "chromo-photography," photographic motion studies that had included, in fact, Eadweard Muybridge's 1887 set of thirty-six sequential photographs called "Nude Woman Descending Stairs."

That February Duchamp submitted *Nude* to the
Salon des Indépendants, run by his brothers' Cubist
friends. Going back to the 1880s, the Salon had a legacy
as an egalitarian, anti-academy venue for artists to freely
show their work under the motto *"sans jury ni récom-
pense"*—"no jury, no prizes." Over the years the Salon
periodically roiled the European art world with wave after
wave of new work—Post-Impressionists, Expressionists,
Symbolists, Fauvists. Now it was the Cubists' time.

The group was dismayed by *Nude*. It was not the
Salon ethos to turn down a submission, especially from
Villon and Duchamp-Villon's little brother, but they did
not like *Nude*. It struck them as "a mockery of Cubist
esthetics," Duchamp would later recall, not to mention
too Futurist (they were feuding with the Futurists). And
there was much too much movement in it. Art nudes were
supposed to recline decorously, not come galumphing
down the stairs like a robot out of control. The day
before the opening, they sent his brothers to speak to
him. " 'The Cubists think it's a little off the beam,' "
he later remembered them saying. " 'Couldn't you at
least change the title?' " The title, which Duchamp had
scrawled across the bottom of the image (a no-no in its
own right), "insinuate[ed] indecency and made it hard to
perceive," art critic Peter Schjeldahl wrote. "[T]he general
idea was to have me change something to make it possible

to show it, because they didn't want to reject it completely," Duchamp went on. "I said all right, all right, and I took a taxi to the show and got my painting and took it away. . . It was a real turning point in my life. I saw that I would never be much interested in groups after that." He later sneered that the Cubists were like "monkeys following the motions of the leader."

As he would do a number of times in his life, Duchamp reacted by running away. He went to Munich, where in two months he made more striking paintings, including *The Passage from the Virgin to the Bride*—which decades later would be the first major Duchamp work to enter the Museum of Modern Art's permanent collection—and one simply titled *Bride*. They were more science-fictionally futuristic than anything the Futurists were doing, and so freely, wildly Cubist that they made Cubists' work look timid.

They can also be considered his last conventional paintings. He was tired of the act of putting paint to canvas. He was running away in a larger sense. The Salon rebuke had genuinely stung him. They didn't like his painting? Well, he didn't like *any* painting! He famously dismissed painting as "retinal," art made just to seduce the eyes. Interviewed in 1946, he would look back and explain

I wanted to get away from the physical aspect of painting. I was much more interested in re-creating ideas in painting . . . I wanted to put painting once again at the service of the mind . . . I was endeavoring to establish myself as far as possible from "pleasing" and "attractive" physical paintings.

In 1913 to '14 he began experimenting with alternatives. For one thing, he began introducing chance into his creative process. In a piece he titled *3 Standard Stoppages*, he dropped lengths of thread onto a canvas, then glued them down in the shapes they made when they landed. It was not exactly accidental art, but he believed he was removing the human touch from it, the painter's recognizable "hand," along with the painter's esthetic choices and tastes. "Forgetting the hand completely, that's the idea," he would say. "When you draw, no matter what you draw, your taste comes in subconsciously . . . I wanted to find something to escape that prison of tradition . . . I unlearned to draw . . . I actually had to forget with my hand." Decades later, his experiments with chance would have a profound influence on the most avant-garde composer in New York, John Cage.

Duchamp also began working out the concept of "readymades," though he wouldn't know that word until he moved to New York. He mounted a bicycle wheel on a stool and called it art. With even less effort, he brought a bottle rack into his studio, put it on the floor, signed it, and called that art too. At this point these were small, private gestures. It wasn't until he was in New York that the idea blossomed into a major challenge to the art establishment.

Meanwhile, when he came back from Munich to Paris he enrolled in a course in library science. "I wanted a nice quiet job that would pay my room and board and let me do what I wanted with my leisure," he later explained. "I was through with the world of the artists, *through*."

Happily, his decision was not so final. When he wasn't at the library, he was plotting one of his most important and revolutionary works, *La Mariée mise à nu par ses célibataires, même*, conventionally rendered in English as *The Bride Stripped Bare by Her Bachelors, Even*. For a man who was resistant to marriage for much of his adult life, brides show up surprisingly often in his work. The piece is also known as *The Large Glass*. Developing it was a process involving years of intense thought and planning. It would be a "painting" on glass, not on canvas, and "painted" with dust and bits of wire, not pigment. He wouldn't start the physical work of making it until he got to New York.

•

Meanwhile, behind his back, he became the star of the Armory Show. With the show, modern art suddenly, explosively, went public in the US, and in a huge way. For one thing, the its sheer size—some 1,400 works by 300 artists—made it the biggest show of its type ever seen in the US, with one-third of its works coming from Europe. And this was no mere art exhibition for an elite of connoisseurs; it was a grand public spectacle with Barnum levels of advance promotion, and the price of admission set at a quarter in the day and a dollar in the evening to keep the show accessible to a wide audience. In its one-month run, some seventy thousand New Yorkers saw it, an astonishing turnout for an art show in its time. "It was the first, and possibly the last, exhibition of paintings held in New York which everybody attended," the writer and scenester Carl Van Vechten declared. He claimed he heard elevator operators, streetcar conductors, and other everyday New Yorkers talking about it.

Following its month in New York, the exhibition traveled to Chicago and Boston, bringing the total attendance to around three hundred thousand. That was truly revolutionary. In a matter of months, looking at fine art had gone from being a delectation for snobs and esthetes to entertainment for the American masses. Decades later, everybody in America knew something about, and had an opinion on, artists like Andy Warhol and Jackson Pollock. Artists had become celebrities. The Armory Show, for better or worse, plowed that field and sowed the seeds.

The Armory Show's notoriety with the general public may be why so many art snobs railed against it. "The thing is pathological! It's hideous!" the National Academy's Kenyon Cox huffed in the *New York Times*. "These men have seized upon the modern engine of publicity and are making insanity pay." One disapproving writer in the *Times* made the essentially correct observation that "Cubists and Futurists are cousins to anarchists," all part of a general movement "to disrupt, degrade, if not destroy, not only art but literature and society too." (Duchamp, who loved puns and wordplay, would take to calling himself "an-artist.") Other critics called the artists "fakers" and, anticipating Nazi jargon, "degenerates."

The press joined in. A photograph of a donkey painting a picture with its tail was reproduced in many newspapers along with a bogus story that it had been exhibited to great praise as avant-garde art. (Some things never change, or only slowly. In 1962 Nikita Khrushchev, leader of the Soviet Union, would revive the slur to rail against the modern art of his era: "A donkey could smear better than that with his tail.") Former president Teddy Roosevelt attended and wrote an article he called a layman's view of the exhibition in *Outlook* magazine. He acknowledged the spirit of change and forward momentum, but he didn't like much of the work anyway. "It is vitally necessary to move forward and to shake off the dead hand of the reactionaries; and yet we have to face the fact that there is apt to be a lunatic fringe among the votaries of any forward movement. In this recent exhibition the lunatic fringe was fully in evidence, especially in the rooms devoted to the Cubists and the Futurists, or Near-Impressionists." Of *Nude*, he said he had a Navajo rug that was better art.

Surprisingly today, Matisse's *Blue Nude* came in for the harshest calumny. Her deathly blue skin and contorted figure horrified and scandalized the experts. They saw her as a mockery and perversion of the hallowed traditions of presenting the female nude in art that stretched back to the Greeks. It was railed at as "epileptic," "depraved," "coarse," "hideous," and "revolting."

Duchamp's *Nude* defied all the traditions too—yet somehow, more than outrage, it seemed to inspire humor. Americans admired this unknown painter's brazen wackiness, his chutzpah, the way they had always admired Barnum. Brown wrote: "There was usually such a crowd before the Duchamp *Nude Descending a Staircase* that it was difficult to see. The buzz of excitement was exhilarating. Some tried to understand, others tried to explain, the great majority either laughed or were infuriated. It could be seen as a symbol of the ultimate in moral degeneracy or as a mad and irresponsible joke. . . . Because of a certain incongruity in its title and the puzzle which it presented, the *Nude* became the focal point of the exhibition. . . . It was the butt of humorous jibes, the object of verse, a puzzle to be deciphered."

A publication called *American Art News* offered a $10 prize to anyone who could find the nude in *Nude*. The winner was a poem:

> You've tried to find her,
> And you've looked in vain
> Up the picture and down again,
> You've tried to fashion her broken bits,
> And you've worked yourself into seventeen fits;
> The reason you failed to tell you I can,
> it isn't a lady but only a man.

Newspaper cartoonists drew parodies like the *Evening Sun*'s "The rude descending a staircase (Rush hour at the subway)." The joke that it looked like "an explosion in a shingle factory" spread widely. A *New York Times* critic decided it was just a hoax.

> M. Duchamp . . . knows perfectly well that there
> is no picture at all—no nude, no staircase, no

anything. Hence must he be having in his heart
much fun with the Wise Ones who, some praising
and some denouncing his work, have insisted that
there is something in it, good or bad, and gravely
have explained or interpreted the artist's meaning
and intention.

Probably responding as much to the publicity as to the
painting itself, a San Francisco art dealer bought *Nude* for
$324. Sales from the show in general went well—at least
for the European works. All the hoopla had stimulated
a sudden hunger for the new among people who could
afford to buy in. To their chagrin, the AAPS artists found
themselves overshadowed. John Quinn, a successful New
York lawyer and political macher, had helped organize
and publicize the show. He spent nearly $6,000 buying
works from it. Quinn was on his way to building a major
collection that included works by Duchamp (an early
painting), both of Duchamp's brothers, and Picasso,
Van Gogh, Matisse, Seurat, Jean-Jacques Rousseau,
Marsden Hartley, and Brâncuși. (He supported modern
literature as well. In 1918 he would defend—unsuc-
cessfully—Margaret Anderson and Jane Heap in their
obscenity trial for serially publishing Joyce's *Ulysses* in
their Greenwich Village magazine *The Little Review*,
the first appearance of the book in print. He also gave

legal advice and financial support to T. S. Eliot and Ezra Pound.)

Walter Arensberg barely made it to the show before it closed, but he came out of the Armory a true believer. He'd missed out on the infamous *Nude*, but he pursued it doggedly and finally became its owner in 1919. He would remain one of Duchamp's most important supporters and boosters until he died in 1954—and in a real sense even afterward.

The wealthy son of a Pittsburgh steel magnate, Walter was no businessman. He was an esthete, a mediocre poet, and writer of arcane "cryptography" books attempting to prove that Francis Bacon wrote Shakespeare's works and that Rosicrucian messages were hidden in Dante's *Inferno*. He now became an impassioned collector and supporter of modern art and artists. He and his wife, Louise, moved from Massachusetts to Manhattan to be at the epicenter of it all.

•

"Flushed with success," Brown wrote, "the Association threw a beefsteak party for its friends and enemies of the press at Healey's Restaurant, 66th St. and Columbus Ave." What was the one artwork reproduced on the invitation? Duchamp's *Nude*. "It was a gay party and the food and drink was served by waitresses who, according to accounts, 'sang and danced.' The participants, not to be outdone, also sang and danced. Sometime during the festivities, speeches were made." A prominent art critic "closed his remarks with a word of praise and admonition, 'It was a good show, but don't do it again.'"

Too late. The Armory Show had catapulted the New York art scene into the modern era. A generation of artists who were painting traditional landscapes before they went to the show woke up Cubists the next morning. All over the city galleries popped up displaying modern work. Soon, World War I would send artists fleeing Europe. Settling in New York City for the duration, they'd help make the city the de facto, if temporary, modern art capital of the world, replacing war-beleaguered Paris.

Today, the first time one sees *Nude* in person—at the Philadelphia Museum of Art, its permanent home since 1954—it can be a surprise in a way not mentioned in 1913. It looms so very large in art history, but it's not very large itself, only about five feet high and three wide. The figure is correspondingly petite. Like some other famous works of art we see lavishly reproduced in art books—the *Mona Lisa* comes to mind—the real thing seems too small to have made such titanic waves.

For his part, Duchamp said he paid very little attention to what was happening in New York in 1913.

He called it "a local success" and said, "I didn't attach much importance to it." All four of his works sold, but the prices were low. He completed his library studies and started work as an intern at the Bibliothèque Sainte-Geneviève in Paris. "It was a wonderful job, because I had so many hours to myself." He used his abundant free time to keep thinking about *The Bride Stripped Bare*.

2 "The Nude-Descending-a-Staircase Man" Arrives

New York itself is a work of art,
a complete work of art.

When Germany declared war on France in August 1914, triggering WWI, France already had a long-standing law conscripting young, fit males for two years' military service. Duchamp's turn had arrived in 1905, when he turned eighteen. He took advantage of a loophole that allowed certain types of workers to serve only a year. He rushed to get a job in a printshop, which allowed him to serve for just one year and remain near his home.

With the start of the war, France began conscripting men by the trainload. Both of Duchamp's brothers were called up. So were Picabia, Léger, and Braque. Apollinaire volunteered. Duchamp, who still owed France another year in uniform, appeared before a draft board in January 1915. He was deferred for a rheumatic heart murmur.

"They found me too *sick* to be a soldier," he commented. "I am not too sad about this decision . . ." He was deeply skeptical of the war. He would tell an American journalist that he found patriotism "absurd" and that "I admire the attitude of combating invasion with folded arms," unintentionally forecasting France's weak response to Hitler's invasion in 1940.

As a young and apparently fit man not in uniform, he became a target of insults. He was even spit at on the street. He decided to run away again—this time to New York. He wrote Walter Pach, who was back in the US: "I do not go there to seek what is missing in Paris. I do not hope to find anything there but individuals . . . I do not go to New York, I leave Paris . . . New York was my only choice because I knew you there. I hope to be able to avoid an artistic life there, possibly with a job that would keep me very busy."

He sailed on June 6, 1915, on an ocean liner, the S.S. *Rochambeau*, that was blacked out because of the threat of U-boats. Half a century later he told the art historian Pierre Cabanne, "When I arrived in New York, I realized that I wasn't a stranger at all." From Cabanne's *Dialogues with Marcel Duchamp*:

Cabanne: You were a man predestined for America.
Duchamp: So to speak, yes.
Cabanne: And you stayed there.

Duchamp: It was like a second wind.

Pach met him when he arrived on June 15 and "arranged for him to move into Walter and Louise Arensberg's large duplex at 33 W. 67th St. The owners were away spending the summer in a rented house in Pomfret, Connecticut," his biographer Calvin Tomkins related.

The neighborhood, called Lincoln Square, was an appropriate place for Duchamp to land. Decades before Lincoln Center was built, it was already a magnet for artists, writers, and musicians, a kind of uptown satellite of Greenwich Village, which was then the artiest and most bohemian neighborhood in America. The block of West 67th Street between Central Park West and 9th Avenue, where the Arensbergs lived, was lined with what were called "studio buildings," purpose-built cooperative housing for artists. The one at 33, completed in 1905, is known as the Atelier. Rather than to struggling bohemians, it catered to successful commercial artists and well-heeled art lovers. One of the Arensbergs' Atelier neighbors was James Montgomery Flagg, who would soon paint the famous 1917 recruitment poster of Uncle Sam (modeled on himself) pointing and declaring "I WANT YOU FOR U.S. ARMY."

When the Arensbergs came home, Duchamp moved to a studio in the nearby Lincoln Arcade building, a barnlike theater-studio-loft space at Broadway and West

65th Street. The Arcade was a micro–Greenwich Village all in itself. Over the years, many artists lived, worked, and caroused in its warren of spaces until it was razed to make way for the Juilliard School. George Bellows and Eugene O'Neill were roommates there. Another Ashcan artist, Robert Henri, had his School for Independent Artists there. The muralist Thomas Hart Benton later remembered being stabbed by an enraged girlfriend there.

If Duchamp had really hoped to stay away from artists it was definitely the wrong place. But it was the right place to work on his own art. As soon as he moved in, he set up sawhorses and laid two large sheets of plate glass across them. After obsessively mulling it over in France, he was now ready to start creating *The Bride Stripped Bare by Her Bachelors, Even*. It seems that getting away from France and coming to New York had freed him.

•

It took until September for the newspapers and magazines to announce that "The Nude-Descending-a-Staircase Man" had come to New York City in the flesh. That month alone he was in the *New York Tribune*, *Vanity Fair*, the *Boston Evening Transcript*, and *Arts & Decoration*. As art historian Dr. Sarah Archino notes, it was the 1910s equivalent of a media blitz.

"The Nude-Descending-a-Staircase Man Surveys
Us" appeared in the *Tribune* that September 12. It ran
below a pro-eugenics think piece by Havelock Ellis. He
postulated that the war was an attempt by nations with
"appalling" high birth rates to purge themselves of "the
weak-minded and reckless lowest social stratum." He
called for "a wise policy of regulative eugenics" instead.
The Nazis would make eugenics abhorrent, but earlier
in the century it was widely embraced by liberals and
humanitarians as a path toward peace and prosperity
for all.

The Duchamp article is more of a puzzler. Bessie
Breuer, the paper's Sunday editor, is believed to have
written it, though it is bylined "by Marcel Duchamp."
For some reason the large photo accompanying the article
shows him reclining decorously in a deck chair, as though
the photographer met him on the *Rochambeau* when it
arrived back in June, which doesn't seem likely—unless
Pach had arranged that too. Breuer fancied the slim,
elegant young Frenchman and became a kind of den
mother to him, showing him around the city.

"The other day I met and talked to the young French
painter at his studio," she (?) wrote. "He is only 28,
dresses most correctly in the mode, and is quite handsome, with blonde curly hair. One would take him for
a well-groomed Englishman rather than a Frenchman."

Why she decided to give him curly blond hair, rather than his actual slicked-back brown hair, is unknown. Nor is it clear how she thought a Frenchman might look, though she did give a hint of how she believed artists acted. "Instead of proving to be a very queer individual, he turned out to be retiring and much more given to listening to the views of those about him than speaking of his own. Just now he is keenly interested in all New York, from the latest musical comedy to Coney Island."

The rest is presented as all Duchamp, translated and doubtless heavily edited. If they really are his words, it was impressive media manipulation on his part, telling the press what they'd want to hear.

"I cannot understand the views my compatriots have expressed about New York," he said. "I know of no city where I would rather be for the next two years—always provided my country does not call me back to it."

And: "The capitals of the Old World have labored for hundreds of years to find that which constitutes good taste and one may say that they have found the zenith thereof. But why do people not understand how much of a bore this is? In Paris, for instance, everything is perfectly blended and in perfect harmony—never in a whole day does one see anything the tiniest bit out of place. But here—from the very instant one lands one realizes that here is a people yearning, searching, trying to find something . . . *If only America would realize that the art of Europe is finished—dead—and that America is the country of the art of the future, instead of trying to base everything she does on European traditions! And yet in spite of it, try as she will, she gets beyond these traditions, even if in dimension alone. Look at the skyscrapers! Has Europe anything to show more beautiful than these?"* (Emphasis added.)

The National Academy's Kenyon Cox, who had reacted so hysterically to the Armory Show, was given a little space for rebuttal. Duchamp "tells us that in America lies the art of the future, and certainly here he is right," he wrote, "but not for the reasons he gives. America is the country of the art of the future, because its art is more classic than any other art today." In other words, American art was the most forward because it was the most backward.

That same month the magazine *Arts & Decoration* ran its own interview with the man of the hour, in which he declared (again, in translation),

New York itself is a work of art, a complete work of art. Its growth is harmonious, like the growth of ripples that come on the water when a stone has been thrown into it. And I believe that your idea of demolishing old buildings, old souvenirs, is fine . . .

The dead should not be permitted to be so much
stronger than the living. We must learn to forget
the past, to live our own lives in our own time.

Duchamp was clearly delighted with all the attention.
He'd been nobody in France. No one from the press
there clamored to interview him. In New York he was
a star. What a fine rebuke to those Cubist monkeys in
Paris. It was America, art historian Moira Roth argues,
"not France, which first created and then maintained
Duchamp's fame . . . From 1913 onwards, the relationship between Duchamp and America became mutually
supportive, positive, and intimate . . . [I]t was America
that provided a home for Duchamp off and on since 1915,
and where his iconoclasm was immediately incorporated
into the history of American modernism . . ." Duchamp's
decision to come to New York, she goes on, "was the
right one for a man obsessed with the making of his
own image, the perpetuation of that image, and the total
control over its reading. Duchamp and America served
one another well. Duchamp wanted fame and got it.
America wanted to establish its place in the history of art
more firmly and it used Duchamp for this purpose."

The conservative art critic Hilton Kramer, writing in
The New Criterion in 1995, put it a different way. "Only
in America was [Duchamp] mistaken to be a major

representative of the modernism that had been created by talents more robust than his. The truth is, the sensation which the *Nude* caused in New York in 1913 was more a reflection of our provincialism than of Duchamp's originality."

•

One day late in 1915 Duchamp went out for a stroll that would change the course of modern art. Again. The Swiss-born French artist Jean Crotti, who was rooming with him for a month at the Arcade, came along. Jean and his wife Yvonne had fled Europe for New York City, a couple of months after Duchamp. Though a newcomer himself, Duchamp had delighted in showing them some of the marvels of Manhattan: the Woolworth Building, completed in 1913 (the tallest building in the world until the Empire State Building was built in 1930–31), drugstore soda fountains pouring egg creams, and Greenwich Village with its bohemians in its faux-French cafés and faux-Italian trattorias.

Duchamp and Crotti walked over to Columbus Avenue, where they saw a hardware store displaying snow shovels. Duchamp later said he'd never seen a snow shovel; they didn't have them in France. He bought one, Crotti threw it over his shoulder, and they marched back to Duchamp's studio. There, along the bottom edge, Duchamp painted its title, *In Advance of the Broken Arm.* He signed and dated it and hung it from the ceiling. And he called it, using the term for the first time, a readymade.

He had started exploring the idea in France with *Bicycle Wheel* and *Bottle Rack.* But from now on he called this particular type of found-object art a readymade, an English word he probably would never have heard if it hadn't "thrust itself upon me," as he put it, in New York City, epicenter of a bustling readymade garment industry. And it was probably only in the US, the world's largest bazaar for mass-produced commercial objects, that he could have refined his thinking about readymades.

For all the impact they would have on future generations of artists, Duchamp treated the readymades at first as private gestures, most often seen only in his studio. Even one of the most famous and infamous readymades, the upended urinal called *Fountain,* was not shown to the public. The public never saw any of them until the 1940s or later, and then it was often replicas, not the originals.

Duchamp considered readymades thought experiments, ways of approaching an answer to a question no one had really thought to raise before his time: *What is art?* Before Duchamp and some of his contemporaries in the Dada movement, everyone assumed they knew the answer. It was simple and obvious. Art was a painting, a drawing, a sculpture. Art was not a bicycle wheel, a snow shovel, a urinal. Readymades asked *Why not?* They started a debate that continued well past their time. Readymades suggested one answer: Art is anything an artist says it is. But it wasn't Duchamp who made that assertion. It was André Breton, in 1938, who defined a readymade as "an ordinary object elevated to the dignity of a work of art by the mere choice of an artist." It's not a definition Duchamp would have given them. Decades later, Andy Warhol, who acknowledged the influence of readymades on his Brillo boxes and soup cans, shrugged, "Art is what you can get away with." He was paraphrasing Marshall McLuhan and Quentin Fiore's *The Medium Is the Massage*, published in 1967, the year before Duchamp died: "Art is anything you can get away with." It was still not quite something Duchamp would have said, but it clearly demonstrated his influence on how art was being thought and talked about.

Duchamp said he hated to repeat himself. "Not to be engaged in any groove is very important for me." He likened it to artistic masturbation. He expressed withering disdain for professional artists who hit on a style that people enjoyed and wanted to buy, and then repeated it for the rest of their careers. Still, he couldn't stop finding excuses to declare some new object a readymade. It amused him. In 1916 he tried to come up with an inscription he could slap on the Woolworth Building so he could declare it a readymade. Sitting in a café with the Arensbergs that year, Duchamp signed the mural on the wall beside them, making it a readymade. He transformed a typewriter cover into a readymade by giving it the title *Traveler's Folding Item*. In a note to himself he speculated that another type of readymade would be to "use a Rembrandt as an ironing-board." And in one of his most famous readymades, when he was back in France in 1919, he gave a reproduction of the *Mona Lisa* a beard and a mustache, appropriating perhaps the most famous art image in the world for a joke, but a thought-provoking one.

Over the years he would often be asked how he chose an object to become a readymade, and he gave various answers. "It's not the visual aspect of the readymade that matters, it's simply the fact that it exists," he once said. "Visuality is no longer a question. The readymade is no longer visible so to speak. It is completely grey matter. *It is no longer retinal*." (Emphasis added.)

From Cabanne's *Dialogues with Marcel Duchamp*:

Cabanne: What determined your choice of readymades?

Duchamp: . . . The choice of readymades is always based on visual indifference and, at the same time, on the total absence of good or bad taste.

Cabanne: What is taste for you?

Duchamp: A habit. The repetition of something already accepted. If you start something over several times, it becomes taste. Good or bad, it's still the same thing, it's still taste.

In another interview, he expanded on that answer. The object, he said, "chooses you, so to speak. If your choice enters into it, then taste is involved—bad taste, good taste, uninteresting taste. Taste is the enemy of art, A-R-T. The idea was to find an object that had no attraction whatsoever from the esthetic angle. *This was not the act of an artist, but of a non-artist, an artisan if you will.* I wanted to change the status of an artist or at least to change the norms used for defining an artist . . . Art, etymologically speaking, means 'to make.' Everybody is making, not only artists, and maybe in coming centuries there will be the making without the noticing." (Emphasis added.)

Asked elsewhere if he thought readymades were art, he said no again, adding, "The fact that they are regarded with the same reference as objects of art probably means I have failed to solve the problem of trying to do away entirely with art."

Then again, to the complaint that a readymade couldn't be art because it was a prefabricated object, Duchamp replied, in a talk he gave at MoMA in 1961, that "all the paintings in the world," since they were made with prefabricated paints from tubes, were ready-mades. That's classic Duchamp, as funny as it is hard to argue against.

•

New York City seemed to heighten a paradox in Duchamp's personal life. On the one hand it detached him from all the roles that would have been assigned to him as a normal middle-class male in France. He embraced his solitude, living a monk's ascetic life, wanting and needing nearly nothing in the way of creature comforts. Although he had many relationships with women, he avoided marriage for a long time and only settled down with his second wife when he was in his sixties. He never had children. He only rarely had what you'd call a job. He spoke explicitly about it. "The things life forces men into—wives, three children, a country house, three cars! I avoid material commitments. I stop. I do whatever life calls me for . . . The artist should be alone . . . Everyone for himself, as in a shipwreck."

At the same time, he loved being known and sought after in New York. When he wasn't alone in his monk's cell, he was out with the crowds, enjoying the raucous, salacious social scenes of Manhattan in that era. He drank too much when he was out partying. His sex life was legendary.

And, for a professed loner, a shipwreck survivor on the sea of life, he made an awful lot of friends in New York. So many of the New Yorkers, and especially New York artists, who met him experienced a *coup de foudre*, instantly attracted to him physically or psychically or both. And they'd stay friends for life.

One of them was Man Ray. In the fall of 1915 Walter Arensberg took Duchamp across the Hudson to visit an artists' colony in Ridgefield, New Jersey, suburbs now, then bucolic countryside. Duchamp had only been in the US for a few weeks and spoke very little English. Man Ray spoke even less French. Adon Lacroix, Man Ray's French-speaking Belgian wife, "acted as my interpreter but mostly carried on a rapid dialogue with [Duchamp]," he recalls in his memoirs, *Self Portrait*. "I brought out a couple of old tennis rackets, and a ball which we batted back and forth without any net, in front of the house. Having played the game on regular courts previously, I called the strokes to make the conversion: fifteen, thirty, forty, love, to which he replied each time with the same word: yes." From this playful, almost silent meeting, Duchamp and Man Ray became friends and collaborators in a relationship that would last the rest of Duchamp's life.

Man Ray was born Emmanuel Radnitzky to Russian Jewish immigrants in Philadelphia in 1890. They moved to Brooklyn when he was seven. Like many Jewish immigrants at the time, they worked in the garment industry. They changed their surname to Ray, common practice among Jews hoping to evade the rampant antisemitism in the US. They nicknamed Emmanuel Manny, and he later shortened it to give himself his decidedly un-Jewish and peerlessly modern-sounding handle. As a young man he haunted 291, where Stieglitz took him under his wing and introduced him to the work of Picasso, Cézanne, Brâncuşi, Rodin. He was one of the many New York artists who woke up the day after the Armory Show painting like a Cubist. He was entirely enthralled by Duchamp. Soon he'd be assisting him with readymades and other projects and making found-object art of his own that looked conspicuously like readymades. He took some of the best-known photos of Duchamp.

Then there was the idiosyncratic painter and authentic eccentric Florine Stettheimer. In *The Life and Art of Florine Stettheimer*, historian Barbara Bloemink writes that the Stettheimer sisters—Florine, her younger sister, Ettie, and older sister, Carrie, collectively known in New York society and art circles as "the Stetties"—"grew up within the hermetic, financially comfortable world of New York's German Jewish society." It was an almost

cartoonish Gilded Age milieu of "quietly ticking
clocks . . . private elevators . . . slippered servants' feet . . .
fires laid behind paper fans." With their mother, who
was abandoned by their wealthy father when they were
growing up, the girls formed a unit that was also, in its
way, hermetically sealed; they've been called a "defensive
phalanx of four." The three sisters always lived together
and never married, though they had their male suitors
and friends. Duchamp would say that they were "inveterate celibates." With their mother they went on extensive
grand tours of Europe, where Florine studied and
absorbed art in Rome, Florence, Paris, Munich.

In 1916, the forty-five-year-old Florine was alone in
New York City for the first time in her life, having left
her mother and sisters vacationing in upstate New York.
She had a studio overlooking Bryant Park where she
slept and worked. She began taking French lessons from
a dashing young man who had arrived from France the
previous year. It was the beginning of a long friendship
with Duchamp. Carrie and Ettie soon joined in the lessons and were as enamored of him as Florine was. He in
turn was clearly very fond of them. For years they formed
a kind of nonsexual ménage à quatre. They affectionately
nicknamed him Duche.

Although Ettie flirted with him the most intensely, of
the three sisters Florine was his true platonic lover. Like

him, she was a staunch solipsist. She wrote a lot of private
poetry. One of her more revealing ditties goes:

> The world is full of strangers
> They are very strange
> I am never going to meet them
> Which I find easy to arrange

They admired each other as artists. By the time she
met Duchamp, Florine had developed a highly individual
style. Her paintings are cartoonlike, frilly, insistently
girly. It would be easy to mistake them as naïve Outsider
art. In fact, she was academically trained and deeply
steeped in art history from all that European travel. She
knew exactly what she was doing when she chose her
style, which has been called "self-administered naïveté."
Her work resembled fashion ads and movie billboards
and *New Yorker* covers more than either the modern
art trends of her day or classical art—although art
historians have seen a resemblance to the over-the-top
exuberance of the Rococo. One early reviewer wrote that
her art looked the way an orchestra sounds when they're
tuning up.

Florine was shy about letting any of those strangers
she wrote about see her work. Duchamp encouraged her
to show it, and, though they worked quite differently

from each other, you can see why. In her own way she was as much an art rebel as he was. And, as much as she held herself apart from the world in her personal life, she, like Duchamp, enthusiastically embraced the Jazz Age culture of New York City with its skyscrapers and tuxes and flappers and commercial hustle. She may have been the only fine artist of her day to exhibit her work at Wannamaker's, the department store, and one of her most fun paintings is *Spring Sale at Bendel's*, another department store. It's no wonder Andy Warhol loved it. ("She's soooo great," he would coo. "Florine Stettheimer is my favorite artist.") As for her naïveté, she did four paintings, called the Cathedrals series, in which there's not a single church; instead she humorously identifies the main religions of the city as money (Cathedrals of Wall Street), show biz (Cathedrals of Broadway), high society (Cathedrals of Fifth Avenue), and the art biz (Cathedrals of Art).

She even painted an outrageous nude of her own. In 1915, at the age of forty-five, she painted her self-portrait, fully naked, reclining like Manet's Olympia, her breasts and pubic area boldly on display. She gazes out of the picture at the viewer with a challenging smile. Like Duchamp's infamous *Nude*, which had arrived in New York only a couple years earlier, this one plays with and confounds hallowed conventions of the art nude, starting with the fact that it is a nude *self-portrait*, a very rare thing for any artist to do, let alone a female one. It was such a daring move that many of her friends failed to recognize the nude as her. They assumed she had hired a model and were discomfited even by that thought.

There was also the irrepressible Beatrice Wood. Born into wealth, artistic and headstrong, she was a constant worry to her parents. In Paris she studied painting, acted with the Comédie-Française, and struggled through her teen years to loosen the ties of her straitlaced upbringing. Back in New York, she continued acting with a French company and took up with the roguish Henri-Pierre Roché. He was a journalist and later novelist (*Jules et Jim*), but his chief occupations seemed to be hanging out with artists and sleeping with as many women as he could. He idolized Duchamp and competed with him for Casanova bragging rights.

Beatrice was twenty-three in the fall of 1916 when, at the urging of a friend, she visited the French avant-garde composer Edgard Varèse, who was lying in St. Vincent's Hospital in Greenwich Village with a broken leg he'd incurred when hit by a taxi. Like Duchamp, he had left France in 1915 to get away from the war. Unlike Duchamp, he was having trouble fitting in. He spoke little English; Beatrice spoke French, hence her visits. He was making a kind of found-object music that was not dissimilar to Duchamp's readymades. "I use streetcar gongs, pipes, bells, and things like that, for it is the music of the city, the soul of the city breaking into sound," he told Beatrice. New York was not getting it at the time. (It would. He subsequently moved permanently to Greenwich Village, and New York would hail him as a genius for both his composing and his conducting.)

"On my third visit to see Varèse my life was to change," Beatrice recorded in her autobiography *I Shock Myself*, "for Marcel Duchamp was there. The most celebrated painter of his day, due to the sensational success of his *Nude Descending a Staircase*, Marcel at twenty-seven had the charm of an angel who spoke slang. He was frail, with a delicately chiseled face and penetrating blue eyes that saw all. When he smiled the heavens opened. But when his face was still it was as blank as a death mask."

Their friendship got off to a bumpy start:

When Marcel and Varèse launched into a discussion on modern art, I shrugged my shoulders and put in: "Anyone can do such scrawls."

Marcel replied wryly: "Try."

He shared his studio with her, as long as she called ahead, in case he had another woman there with him. "Marcel did very well in that department, although

friends laughingly told me that Marcel's lady friends
were usually quite homely. Marcel later commented that
unattractive women made love better than beautiful
ones. Sex and love, he explained, were two very different
things. I did not know what he was talking about."

Like everyone who visited him, Beatrice was struck by
his spartan living condition.

> Marcel's square room looked out onto a narrow
> court, facing the back of the apartment. A double
> bed, usually unmade, filled one alcove. There were
> two chairs generally covered with clothes and
> canvases in disorder everywhere. On the window-
> sill lay boxes of crackers and packages of Swiss
> chocolate, his regular diet. The room gave the
> impression of being in various stages of undress . . .
> After the crowded luxury of my parents' home, I
> found this chaotic space an oasis of peace.

Soon he'd help her make a piece of art that rattled the
New York art scene almost as much as his own work had.

3 Fountain

America likes and demands clean art.

Marcel, Marcel, I love you like hell, Marcel.

In the handful of years leading up to the US entering the Great War, roughly 1912 into 1917, Greenwich Village became acknowledged around the world as the Left Bank of America, its largest enclave of artists, intellectuals (a relatively new coinage then), radicals, and bohemians. Villagers played key roles in organizing the Armory Show in 1913. Eugene O'Neill, Djuna Barnes, Mabel Dodge, Edna St. Vincent Millay, Hart Crane, Theodore Dreiser, John Reed, Upton Sinclair, Emma Goldman, Margaret Sanger, and others put the Village on the leading edge of new culture and politics. The candle burned brightly but briefly; by the 1920s people would already be looking back on it as Greenwich Village's "golden age." That was premature, but it suggests what a momentous few years it had been.

The Village in these years attracted like-minded individuals from literally everywhere. Although he wouldn't live there until the 1940s, Duchamp was naturally drawn to it. On a cold night in January 1917 six revelers snuck into the Washington Square Arch after noticing that the door at the base had been left unlocked, and climbed the spiral stairs to the top, which was decidedly off-limits. The Arch, erected in Washington Square in 1892, was by then considered a symbol of everything old and stodgy and self-important. Henry James had called it "the lamentable little Arch of Triumph." These partiers included Duchamp, the painter John Sloan (at forty-five, the oldest of the group), a trio of actors from the Provincetown Playhouse, which had just landed on nearby MacDougal Street in 1916, and the ringleader, Gertrude Drick, a vivacious young blonde recently arrived from Texas. She'd been drawn to the Village as a budding artiste, but after failing as a musician, poet, and painter, she'd settled for being one of the Village's colorful hipsters. Before this night she was best known for handing out a black-edged calling card with "Woe" printed on it so she could say, "Woe is me."

They got a little campfire going in a pot, strung Chinese lanterns and balloons from the parapet, ate a picnic of sandwiches and wine, and then, as the others fired off cap pistols, Drick read a declaration of independence for "the Republic of Greenwich Village," its secession from the rest of the United States. It consisted of a single word repeated over and over: "Whereas . . . Whereas . . . Whereas . . ." Sloan made a nice etching he called *Arch Conspirators*, memorializing the night, showing them huddled like hobos around their small fire.

It was a classically nonsensical Dada event. But beneath its surface nonsense and frivolity, Dada carried the purpose of a deeper rebellion. As of January 1917 the Great War in Europe, begun in August 1914, had slogged on for well more than two years. The US would finally be dragged into it the coming April. For all its evident silliness, Dada was a cri de coeur, a shout of revulsion against the old order and corrupt logic that had led to horrific slaughter. After his humiliation at the hands of the Cubists, Duchamp never fully embraced Dada or the Surrealism movement it morphed into, jealously guarding his individuality. But he had many Dada and Surrealist friends—Picabia, Apollinaire, Breton, Tristan Tzara, and others—and *they* embraced Duchamp wholeheartedly. He was a hero to them, a god, the greatest provocateur of them all. Breton and Apollinaire practically swooned on the page rhapsodizing about him. "Can it be that Marcel Duchamp arrives more quickly than anyone else at the *critical point* of an idea?" Breton wondered. Apollinaire mused, "It is perhaps reserved for an artist so detached

from esthetic preoccupations, so preoccupied with energy
as Marcel Duchamp, to reconcile Art and the People."
Many years later, in 1952, *Life* magazine would declare
Duchamp "Dada's Daddy."

In the spring of 1917 he demonstrated why.

•

Since they moved to New York, the Arensbergs had
been hosting nightly salons at the duplex in the Atelier
that attracted the cream of Manhattan's modernists.
Duchamp was a star figure as soon as he began to attend,
even though, according to Man Ray, he most often sat
in a corner and played chess. Beatrice Wood did the
same the following year. Any given night Joseph Stella
might also be there, Isadora Duncan, William Carlos
Williams, George Bellows, Walter Pach, Carl Van
Vechten, the poet-and-scenester Mina Loy. "How would
the modernizing New York art world have evolved had
the Arensbergs not existed—or if Duchamp hadn't made
his way to their door?" art critic Peter Schjeldahl once
pondered. "Differently, for sure, and with considerably
less social synergy."

It was at the Arensbergs', at the end of 1916, that
members of this group decided to form the Society
of Independent Artists. Founding members included

Walter Arensberg, Pach, Man Ray, Stella, Bellows, and Duchamp. John Quinn provided legal advice. Besides Arensberg, wealthy New Yorkers who donated financial supported included Vanderbilts, Whitneys, and, most notably, Katherine Dreier. Born into a well-off household in Brooklyn Heights, Dreier was a painter and dedicated collector of the new art; in 1913 she had loaned the Armory Show a Van Gogh. Like so many, she was taken with Duchamp from the instant she met him. They formed a long collaborative bond, another of his platonic relationships that seem more sturdy than his romantic and erotic ones. They were important for each other in a number of ways until she died in 1952.

The society's plan was to stage exhibitions modeled on the Salon des Indépendants in Paris. Any artist who paid five dollars in annual dues and a one dollar entry fee could show two works. As in Paris, there would be "no jury, no prizes." The idea took off with artists eager to show that their work was as good as any Picasso or Matisse. It didn't hurt that with the war devastating Europe and the Atlantic infested with U-boats, not much new work was coming from Over There. "Within two weeks of the first announcement, the society had six hundred members" from around the country, Tomkins reported. They booked a space for their first exhibition in the new (1911) Grand Central Palace, a Beaux arts behemoth that was on Lexington Avenue, as the Armory Show had been, but this was twenty blocks uptown, between 46th and 47th Streets.

From the start, Duchamp showed his Puckish trickster side. With his humiliating rejection from the Paris Salon des Indépendants still fresh in his memory, he kept challenging this group to prove that they could be as egalitarian in deed as in words, and they kept failing. He caused his first stir when he declared, as the leader of the picture-hanging committee, that the paintings be hung alphabetically by the artists' surnames. The point was to eliminate any personal preferences or esthetic judgments in determining which paintings were hung where. And, to add an element of chance, he wrote the letters of the alphabet on slips of paper, scrambled them in a hat, and pulled out one, the letter *R*. So, as exhibit goers entered the hall, they'd first see all the paintings by artists whose last names began with *R*, then all the *S* artists, and so on through the alphabet, until they finally reached the *Q*s.

The society was disconcerted. Robert Henri quit the show in a huff over it. Quinn called it "democracy run riot." This becomes hilarious, Duchamp scholar Francis Naumann writes, given that four days before the exhibition opened on April 10, President Woodrow Wilson took the US into the European war he'd been avoiding since 1914, with the express purpose of preserving democracy.

So, first round to Duchamp. A Frenchman had challenged the Americans on their devotion to democracy, and the Americans, or some of them anyway, lost.

His next gambit has gone down in the history books as a pivotal moment in twentieth-century art. The art historian William A. Camfield called it "one of the most famous and/or infamous objects in the history of modern art." Schjeldahl said it was Duchamp's "inception of what amounted to a Copernican revolution in art, from a secure set of disciplines to an unmoored category of anything an artist might say it is." It generated controversy that continues to this day, more than a century later.

There are two basic versions of the *Fountain* story, one essentially pro-Duchamp and one anti-Duchamp. This is the first version:

Determined to push the society harder to prove its democratic ideals, Duchamp took Arensberg and Man Ray to the J. L. Mott plumbing supply showroom on Fifth Avenue at 17th Street, where he bought a white porcelain urinal. At his studio he stood it on its back. In this position it looked something like a smooth, modernist Brâncuși sculpture, maybe a Madonna or a Buddha. Duchamp signed it in crudely painted lettering *R. MUTT 1917*. Decades later he said that this referred to the newspaper comic strip *Mutt & Jeff*.

"Two days before the official opening," Tomkins wrote, "this object was delivered to the Grand Central Palace, together with an envelope bearing the fictitious Mr. Mutt's six-dollar membership and entry fee and the work's title: *Fountain*." Beatrice Wood recounted in her memoirs that she came upon George Bellows and Walter Arensberg that day standing by *Fountain*, which was on the floor between them, and arguing fiercely. Bellows's Ashcan School paintings were about as avant-garde as American art got before 1913, and evidently as far as he thought it should go.

> *"We cannot exhibit it," Bellows said hotly, taking out a handkerchief and wiping his forehead.*
>
> *"We cannot refuse it, the entry fee has been paid," gently answered Walter.*
>
> *"It is indecent!" roared Bellows.*
>
> *"That depends upon the point of view," added Walter, suppressing a grin.*

Bellows continued to bellow, Arensberg to quietly differ. Increasingly frustrated, Bellows shouted:

> *"You mean to say, if a man sent in horse manure glued to a canvas that we would have to accept it!"*
>
> *"I'm afraid we would," said Walter, with a touch of undertaker sadness. "If this is an artist's*

*expression of beauty, we can do nothing but accept
his choice.”*

Eight decades later, Mayor Rudolph Giuliani would
have a very similar fight with the Brooklyn Museum
over Chris Ofili's painting *The Holy Virgin Mary*, which
incorporated elephant dung.

The shouting continued.

*“It is gross, offensive! There is such a thing as
decency.”*

*“Only in the eye of the beholder. You forget our
bylaws.”*

The matter was referred to the society's whole board
of directors, who voted, by a slim margin, to reject the
piece. Arensberg and Duchamp instantly resigned. Twice
now Duchamp had challenged the society he had helped
create to live up to its stated ideals, and twice it had
failed. *He had been ejected from his own exhibition.*

We'll never know how the board would have voted if
they knew that it was the most celebrated artist in their
ranks who had submitted the piece. Duchamp later said
that his "testing of the 'no jury' policy would have been
compromised" if they knew *Fountain* came from him. It
was seventeen years before he publicly claimed *Fountain*

as his. In 1917 only Arensberg, Man Ray, Wood, and Roché were in on the prank.

Or . . . maybe not. In *toutfait*, the journal of Duchamp studies, the art historian Michael Betancourt raised the interesting notion that Bellows may have known, or at least suspected, that R. Mutt was Duchamp. In his *Self Portrait*, Man Ray recalls an evening at Arensberg's duplex "filled with his collection of moderns. There was a mixed crowd; Picabia from France, various women and Duchamp, who sat quietly in a corner playing chess with a neurologist. *George Bellows, the painter, walked around with a disdainful and patronizing air, evidently out of place in the surroundings.*" (Emphasis added.) Bellows might have known and disapproved of Duchamp's readymades. His outrage would then take on a more personal tinge: He was angry *with Duchamp* for insulting him and the society with this prank.

The most succinct defense of *Fountain* ever written was published that May in a small pamphlet called *The Blind Man*. It was created by Duchamp, Roché, and Wood, who got in trouble with her father when he saw it and realized the type of people with whom she was consorting. Walter Arensberg's address was its mailing address. The eight-page volume 1 came out April 10, the day the exhibition opened, to little fanfare.

Then *Fountain* happened, and the trio put out volume 2 (the last volume) the next month. It had twice as many pages, and it contained an unsigned editorial, probably written by Wood with Duchamp's approval:

The Richard Mutt Case

They say any artist who pays six dollars may exhibit.

Mr. Richard Mutt sent in a fountain. Without discussion, this object disappeared and was never exhibited.

What were the grounds for refusing Mr Mutt's fountain:—

1. Some contended it was immoral, vulgar.

2. Others that is was plagiarism, a plain piece of plumbing.

Now Mr. Mutt's fountain is not immoral, that is absurd, no more than a bath tub is immoral. It is a fixture which you see every day in plumbers' show windows.

Whether Mr. Mutt with his own hands made the fountain or not has no importance. He CHOSE it. He took an ordinary article of life, placed it so that its useful significance disappeared under the new title and point of view—created a new thought for that object.

As for plumbing, that is absurd. The only works of art America has produced are her plumbing and her bridges.

As a rationale for found-object art, taking "an ordinary article of life" and creating "a new thought for that object" works pretty well for everything from *Fountain* and the other readymades to Robert Rauschenberg's Combines, Warhol's Brillo boxes, Jeff Koons's floating basketballs and Michael Jacksons, and Conceptual art, Minimalist art, and Postmodern art.

The editorial was accompanied by a photo of *Fountain* taken by Alfred Stieglitz in 291, at Duchamp's request. Beatrice Wood wrote that Stieglitz "was greatly amused, but also felt that it was important to fight bigotry in America. He took great pains with the lighting." This familiar shot is all we have of *Fountain*, because Stieglitz closed 291 soon after, and the urinal was never seen again. There have been many replicas, but the original may well have been tossed out when Stieglitz vacated the space. It didn't matter. The entire point of *Fountain* was that the importance was not the object but the idea, the gesture, and the reactions the idea prompted.

•

That's the generally accepted version of the *Fountain* story. It's been challenged by an alternative history. Though widely dismissed, this other version does contain a few compelling if not dispositive elements. It merits at least a digression.

In this version, *Fountain* wasn't Duchamp's "new thought." It was Baroness Elsa von Freytag-Loringhoven's. Baroness Elsa was one of the most outrageous figures on the New York arts scene in the 1910s. Everyone wrote about her. She's Frau Mann, the Duchess of Broadback in Djuna Barnes's *Nightwood*. Margaret Anderson, cofounder of *The Little Review*, told several wild stories about her in her autobiography *My Thirty Years' War*. No arts ball was safe from an outlandish, usually uninvited appearance by her. Everybody drew and painted and photographed her. Women admired her raw sexuality. Men fled from it. In recent years, art historians have been renovating her reputation, identifying her not just as an eccentric fringe figure but as a pioneering avant-gardist and Dadaist. If Duchamp is Dada's Daddy, they say, the Baroness is Dada's Mama.

In her 2002 biography *Baroness Elsa*, the scholar Irene Gammel pieced together a portrait from the fragments of Elsa's chaotic life. She was born Else Plötz in 1874 in a small German town. As a teenager she escaped her abusive household for Berlin, home to a vibrant arts scene in the 1890s, where she studied art, cultivated androgynous fashions, posed in flesh-colored tights for racy vaudeville tableaux, was a chorus girl, and threw herself into a whirlwind of sexual relations that left her with syphilis, which may explain why in her later years she was said to be "unhampered by sanity." Syphilis was extremely resistant to known treatments before the discovery of penicillin, and often led to dementia.

Elsa and her second husband, the novelist Felix Paul Greve, lived and traveled on money given to him by a former gay lover, who then had Greve jailed for a year on fraud charges. In 1909, to escape crushing debts, Elsa and Greve faked his suicide and fled to the US, ending up in rural Kentucky, where he abandoned her. In 1913 she made her way to New York City, arriving at the same time that modern art did at the Armory. That year she met and soon married the German Baron Leopold von Freytag-Loringhoven. She was thirty-nine, gave her age as twenty-eight on the marriage license, and concealed that she was still married to Greve. Leo was twenty-eight, a former army officer and fallen scion of a noble house. They honeymooned at the Ritz, then he returned to his job as a busboy. When the Great War broke out the next year he sailed to Europe to fight for Germany. His ship was taken by the French before it reached harbor, and he sat out the war a prisoner. He never fired a shot until 1919, when he put a bullet through his brain.

When Duchamp arrived in 1915, the Baroness was working as a life model at the Art Students League and elsewhere, earning a desperate dollar an hour. She "lived in total disorder in the Lincoln Arcade building with an assortment of animals, mostly mangy dogs and cats," according to Gammel. This makes her a neighbor of Duchamp's from 1915 into 1916, when he was a new-comer to the city. She and Duchamp began a precarious friendship. (All her friendships were precarious.) She ferociously loved and lusted after him. Once, when a friend showed her a newspaper clipping about *Nude*, she "took the clipping and gave herself a rubdown with it, missing no part of her anatomy. The climax was a poem she had composed for Duchamp. It went 'Marcel, Marcel, I love you like hell, Marcel.'"

He, despite all the other women he slept with, firmly resisted her carnal advances. Being fastidious himself, he may well have been repelled by her notorious lack of hygiene, much commented on by others. William Carlos Williams, whom she also lusted after, poetically lamented that "a reek stood out purple from her body." He once punched her in the mouth to keep her at bay. Duchamp was, however, very attracted to her as a wild, anarchic force in art. "She is not a futurist," he once said. "She is the future." She must have agreed. She wrote that he was a futurist but she herself was a "future futurist."

Regarding Elsa and *Fountain*, the first interesting fact is that in 1913, on her way to City Hall to marry poor

Baron Leopold, she found "an iron ring on the street that she claimed as a female symbol representing Venus. This was her first found object used as art," Gammel relates. So she was already making her version of a readymade two years before Duchamp arrived. Over time she took to wearing found objects in elaborate costumes. Margaret Anderson recalled that when Elsa first walked into the *Little Review*'s office she was wearing a bolero jacket, a kilt, spats, a multitude of dime-store bracelets, two old tea balls hanging from her breasts, and a black tam-o'-shanter with ice-cream spoons dangling from it. For hats she wore peach baskets, wastepaper baskets, and, once, a wedding cake. She attended a costume ball wearing parrot feather eyelashes and wouldn't leave the stage until she was awarded a prize. At a reception for a famous opera diva, "One side of her face was decorated with a canceled postage stamp," Anderson wrote. "Her lips were painted black, her face powder was yellow. She wore the top of a coal scuttle for a hat, strapped on under her chin like a helmet. Two mustard spoons at the side gave the effect of feathers." She was a walking readymade.

It's also interesting that in 1917, the year of *Fountain*, when she had briefly fled New York for Philadelphia, she mounted a twisty length of iron pipe she'd found and titled it *God*. Was it a coincidence that she and Duchamp were simultaneously declaring that bits of plumbing were art?

Then there's a letter Duchamp wrote to his sister the day after the exhibition opened, containing the curious line: "One of my female friends under a masculine pseudonym, Richard Mutt, sent in a porcelain urinal as a sculpture . . ." Those who ascribe *Fountain* to Duchamp have always had trouble explaining away this line. Proponents of the Baroness theory contend that it's obvious: she was the female friend. She found the urinal in Philadelphia, where, they claim, that particular brand of urinal was on display, not in New York. She signed it R. Mutt as a play on the German word *Armut* (poverty), decrying her chronic lack of funds, and sent it to be submitted in the exhibition. Duchamp recognized it as her work, and when it was rejected he resigned in solidarity with an artist he admired.

Baroness fans also note that Duchamp did not start to claim *Fountain* as his work until 1934, after she had died in Paris in 1927. As the decades went by and *Fountain* was hailed as a watershed in modern art, he seemed increasingly willing to be solely identified with it. The Baroness died in wretched circumstances, having left the gas on in her room as she went to sleep. It's unclear whether she'd intended suicide or was merely careless. In the most extreme version of this alternate history, it was neither: Duchamp murdered her, or at least arranged for her murder, to keep his secret safe forever. In this version, his alter ego Rrose Sélavy, who started showing up in his work in 1920, is a loose anagram for Sorry, Elsa.

The irreverence that produced *Fountain*—art you piss on, art that grins and gives the finger to arty pretention—is an attitude Duchamp and Elsa shared. And one final note. It's known that Duchamp was not above exploiting Elsa's mad wantonness for his own purposes. In 1921 he and Man Ray made a short film, *Elsa, Baroness von Freytag-Loringhoven, Shaving Her Pubic Hair.* They wrecked it in the editing process, but Duchamp salvaged a single frame. It was an image of Elsa's legs spread wide, showing off her vagina, which he reproduced as a sort of logo—and which seems a lot like a foreshadowing of the shocking spread-eagle nude in his last work, *Étant donnés.*

•

"The Big Show," as one participating artist called it, opened on April 10, 1917, with some 2,125 paintings and sculptures by 1,235 artists from thirty-eight states. At Duchamp's urging, Florine Stettheimer had two works in the show.

"Thousands gathered to celebrate what was to be the largest art exhibition ever held in New York—almost twice the size of the famous Armory Show four years earlier," Francis Naumann relates. "Nearly everyone associated with the New York art scene made an appearance—from the crudely clad, long-haired artists of lower Washington Square to the starch-fronted academicians accompanied by their consorts in formal evening dress and opera gowns." They "spent the evening strolling up and down the endless avenues formed by large temporary partitions set up between the classical columns of the palace, upon which hung a myriad of confusing submissions. It was even reported that a fleet of wheelchairs was hired to save fatigue and, as one reporter put it, in order 'to get by the terrible works quickly.'" Journalists and some critics proved themselves as resistant to the new as they'd been four years earlier. One Brâncuşi sculpture, which was undeniably phallic despite being titled *Princess Bonaparte*, was condemned by a journalist who flatly declared, "America likes and demands clean art." We can guess what he would have made of *Fountain*.

Duchamp was far from done with his provocations. One of the works critics found most upsetting in the show was a painting by Beatrice Wood she'd titled, in mangled French, *Un peu d'eau dans du savon*—A little water in soap. She'd meant to correct it to *Un peu de savon dans l'eau*, but Duchamp, a fan of spoonerisms, told her to keep it. It depicted a female nude in a bath with a bar of soap covering her pubic area. "You must put a soap there, real soap, instead of painting it," she recalled him insisting. She bought a scallop-shaped bar of soap, and they glued it to the nude's crotch. It was another classic Duchamp provocation, elevating, by one simple gesture, an unremarkable and innocent artwork into a focus of intense interest and controversy. "To my astonishment," Wood recounted, "the painting, perhaps the first assemblage or abstraction by an American to be put on public view, attracted more attention than any other entry. Crowds stood in front of it chuckling, men left their calling cards, and the reviews gave it more space than that given to serious artists who truly deserved it."

Forcibly drawing the viewer's eye to the female's pubic area while ostentatiously hiding it—"insinuating indecency and making it hard to perceive"—made the work seem far more prurient than a simple nude would have been. Like his *Nude* and Matisse's *Blue Nude* four years earlier, it was denounced as a mockery and desecration of the long tradition of honoring the female body in art. "Marcel was delighted that his prankishness had come home to roost, and the harsh reviews pleased him all the more."

Duchamp still wasn't done poking. When the press asked him to name his favorite works in the show, he cited Louis Eilshemius's *Supplication*, a painting of an ungainly, zaftig nude cavorting in nature. Eilshemius was

well known in New York art circles, not so much as an
artist but as a crank and a pest. Like Florine Stettheimer,
he was academy trained, but with his idiosyncrasies, he
could be mistaken for an amateur or Outsider artist.
He had tried and failed to get into the Armory Show.
Convinced of his genius, he constantly harangued critics
and academics for not agreeing with him. He valued
Supplication at $15,000, the highest price for a painting
in the show. Over time, his delusions of grandeur went
cosmic and he would award himself titles like Mightiest
Man, Mahatma, and Wonder of the Worlds. All of which
no doubt endeared him to Duchamp. "Duchamp's name
was associated with the most advanced level of modern
taste," Naumann wrote, "and a nod of approval from
him was taken seriously, despite the numerous reserva-
tions that critics immediately expressed." Duchamp's
friend Katherine Dreier would give Eilshemius his
first solo exhibition in 1920. Other galleries and
museums followed.

Duchamp played one more trick on the society: he
unleashed Arthur Cravan on them. A nephew of Oscar
Wilde (whom he never met), born and raised in Switzerland, Cravan was big, built like an athlete, handsome,
and thoroughly enamored with himself. He was a poet,
a pugilist—Jack Johnson, well past his prime, knocked
him out in a highly touted match in Spain in 1916—and a

massive drunk. He had a penchant for being at the center
of outrageous spectacles that the Dadaists admired.

In January 1917 Cravan landed in New York City on
the same ship that brought Leon Trotsky and his family
to the US. Trotsky had been exiled from Spain; Cravan
was evading military service in the war. They struck up
an unlikely shipboard friendship but parted ways in the
city. Trotsky stayed in New York for ten weeks, Cravan
for under ten months.

When Picabia and Duchamp learned Cravan was
in town they enlisted him to give a lecture on art for
the exhibition. It's said that they got him very drunk
beforehand. Years later, Picabia's wife Gabriëlle recalled:
"Cravan arrived very late, pushing his way through the
large crowd of very smart [i.e., smartly dressed] listeners.
Obviously drunk, he had difficulty in reaching the
lecture platform, his expression and gait showing the
decided effects of alcohol. He gesticulated wildly and
began to take off his waistcoat . . . After having taken
off his waistcoat, he began to undo his suspenders. The
first surprise of the public at his extravagant entrance was
soon replaced by murmurs of indignation. Doubtless the
authorities had already been notified, for, at that moment,
as he leaned over the table and started hurling one of the
most insulting epithets in the English language at his
audience, policemen attacked him suddenly from behind

and handcuffed him with professional skill. He was manhandled, dragged out, and would have been thrown into jail, but for the intervention of Walter Arensberg, who bailed him out and took him to his house . . . What a wonderful lecture, said Marcel Duchamp, beaming, when we all met that evening at the home of Arensberg."

The Big Show drew an estimated twenty thousand visitors and a lot of press, though few works sold and critics found it all too uneven and unwieldy. The Society of Independent Artists would continue on without the bothersome Duchamp, holding annual exhibitions into 1944.

Fountain may have disappeared, but as the arguably best known of the readymades, it "lit a long fuse for concatenating detonations in future artistic and intellectual culture," Schjeldahl wrote. The critic Brooks Adams declared, "Duchamp's readymades redefined the course of modern art. After the urinal, anything and everything was admissible *materiel* for painting and sculpture. The ensuing history of the century can be seen as an exploration, and an explosion, of the idea of what constitutes art."

•

On July 28, 1917, the Stetties invited a dozen friends to their summer house up the Hudson for a party. It was

Duchamp's thirtieth birthday. Guests included Picabia, of whom Ettie disapproved, calling him "a fat womanish enfant terrible, self-centered Bohemian with a high power automobile in which he and Duche came out later than anyone else." The ubiquitous Carl Van Vechten came, and Gertrude Stein's brother Leo, and Isadora Duncan's sister, Elizabeth. Florine Stettheimer memorialized it in a painting, *La Fête à Duchamp*. Among the guests all cavorting decorously on the lawn, she shows Duchamp in three places at once, maybe as a winking reference to *Nude*. When he reviewed the painting, the witty art critic Henry McBride wrote, "Miss Stettheimer appears to be a good provider. The more I think of it, the more miffed I am that I wasn't asked to that party."

•

One indication of how fond Duchamp was of Katherine Dreier is that in 1918 he agreed to paint her a painting to go over a bookcase in her home. He had renounced painting on canvas and had not made one for four years. Plus, this one had to be a weirdly long and narrow strip, 10 feet long and 2.3 feet high. But he did it, and the result, called *Tu m'*, is another of his idiosyncratic masterpieces, so sumptuously "retinal" it seems a betrayal of his cause, yet very Duchampian in execution. It incorporates the sketched shadows of a bicycle wheel and other self-referential objects; a line of almost op-art diamond shapes in bright colors that visually zoom out of the canvas toward the viewer as in a 3D movie; a trompe l'oeil rip in the canvas that's held together by real safety pins; and a bottle-washing brush that actually juts out of the canvas almost 2 feet. For all his renouncing "retinal" art, *Tu m'* is a sumptuous feast for the eyes.

Duchamp got a professional sign painter to add a pointing hand. Distancing himself from the whole thing, he had this person, A. Klang, sign it instead of him. *Tu m'* stands for "tu m'ennuies" or "tu m'emmerdes," a vulgar way of saying "You bore me" or "You annoy me." Was he addressing Dreier? Maybe. Himself? Maybe. The act of painting? Almost certainly. It was the last time he ever painted on canvas. And yet, as Brooks Adams argued toward the end of the twentieth century, it "strikes one as the seminal work, one that may supersede even [*The Bride Stripped Bare*] in contemporary relevance." For the generation who rediscovered Duchamp in the 1960s—Rauschenberg, Jasper Johns, and others—it was the inspiration for all manner of assemblage-construction-paintings. As well as, Adams wrote, "a prototype of postmodern painting in all its tropes and guises, at once figurative and abstract, mundane and arcane, advanced and retardataire."

•

And then, seemingly out of nowhere, Duchamp announced his intention to leave New York and sail to Buenos Aires. One interpretation of this sudden and drastic move is that, always the escape artist, he wanted to distance himself from the war as he had when he fled France in 1915; he was feeling stifled by the patriotic war fever that swept up New York—marches, speeches, recruiting stations sprouting up all over the city—when the US entered the war in April 1917. Argentina was far from the war, a neutral country. Or maybe he had found himself in a rut artistically, bored with himself (*Tu m'*), hoping to find new inspiration in a place that he knew nothing about. "The advantage is that it's far away," he wrote to Picabia. He also quipped, "Buenos Aires does not exist." He was running away again.

Jean and Yvonne Crotti, now divorced, had returned to New York City in January 1918. She was now using her maiden name, Yvonne Chastel. She and Duchamp soon started sleeping together. He now asked her to sail to Argentina with him. But he also asked Ettie Stettheimer, which bemused her. Calvin Tomkins records:

"Duche expects to leave for Buenos Aires next month," [Yvonne] wrote in her journal in July, "but I couldn't make out why—excepting that he doesn't think he's happy here anymore. He asked me to go with him 3 times! Whatever that expressed I don't know . . . Poor little floating atom, a strange boy. —But a dear."

Meanwhile Duchamp also sent Florine a wistfully melancholy drawing that showed North and South America and the route he'd sail. The Stettheimers' house up the Hudson dominated the northern continent. A giant question mark hovered over Buenos Aires. He wrote "1915–1918" and "two years and twenty-seven days"—how long he'd been in New York. At the bottom he signed it "Adieu a Florine, Marcel Duchamp, 13 August 1918." Leaving New York had been his idea, but he couldn't have seemed more conflicted about it.

He and Yvonne Chastel sailed for Buenos Aires. There he lost himself in constant chess playing. Yvonne got bored and left him, sailing to France. He worked little on his art while there, though he did finish the beautifully odd glass piece with the exhaustingly precise title/direction, *To Be Looked at (from the Other Side of the Glass) with One Eye, Close to, for Almost an Hour*. He had no contact with local artists in the city, but later, in the 1960s and '70s, the Latin American Conceptual art movement would look to him both for inspiration and as a foil.

Duchamp stayed only nine months in Argentina. Whatever he thought he was going there to find, if anything, he didn't. By June 1919 he was sailing for France. He'd been away from there for four years. But then, finding war-ravaged Europe an unhappy place to be, he fled yet again and sailed back to New York that December.

4 Escape from New York

M. Duchamp is really too daring.

> *With consistency a great soul*
> *has simply nothing to do.*

Duchamp arrived back in New York on January 6, 1920.
Prohibition arrived on January 17. "One doesn't drink
here anymore and it's quiet, too quiet," he wrote to
Yvonne Chastel in France. He returned to the Lincoln
Arcade and had *The Bride Stripped Bare* brought there
from the Arensbergs'. They had been storing it for him.

They were no longer hosting their salon; Walter,
the classic rich man's son with no head for finance, had
spent down much of his inheritance on art and was
preoccupied with his project to decode Shakespeare. In
1921 they would visit Hollywood, and soon, at Louise's
insistence, moved there permanently. She was convinced
that Walter's health required getting him out of the hectic
Manhattan scene and into a more relaxed life. They took

their extensive modern art collection, including their Duchamps, with them. Duchamp was not happy about it. He didn't like having a key source of both moral and financial support so far away, or his artworks either.

His work on *The Bride* did not proceed quickly or diligently. He let it sit for months gathering dust, which he'd fix with varnish. Having given up on applying paint to canvas, he was now "painting" with dust on glass. He had thought and written so very much about the thing that actually creating it must have felt anticlimactic and superfluous. The ideas were what mattered to him, he always insisted, and the ideas were all written down on many slips of paper, a hermetic cosmos that scholars and fans have endeavored to decipher and interpret ever since.

It was at the dust-gathering stage when Man Ray saw it. He and Duchamp had resumed their friendship as soon as Duchamp returned to New York. They would meet in the evenings at the Pepper Pot, the famous café on West 4th Street below the Marshall Chess Club, favored by both chess players and Village bohemians. Duchamp would have his usual frugal meal, and then they'd go upstairs and he'd play chess all night. Man Ray liked hanging out there because "[t]here were pretty girls who brought one coffee; the place was a mixture of sociability and serious players," he recalled.

Duchamp's obsession with chess has been the topic of intense study. He started playing with his brothers when he was a kid and never stopped. Chess features as a motif in much of his work. He invented a pocket chess set, played games by telegram, and co-wrote a treatise on the game. He won some tournaments and was designated a master by the French Chess Federation. According to Man Ray, at the start of Duchamp's inexplicable six-month marriage in France in 1927, his wife Lydie would get so frustrated with his playing chess all night rather than celebrating their honeymoon that she glued his chess pieces to the board. Lydie later denied it. (He was forty, she was twenty-four. For him, it may have been an experiment in settling down and accepting the bourgeois life he'd been avoiding. He was quickly bored and coldly left her.) The more unhappy he was with the art world, the more he turned to chess as a refuge.

On one level, it may simply be that like other addicted hobbyists who are only happy when golfing or gaming, Duchamp liked it so much because he got very good at it. He had satisfying victories in the field when the art world was mostly disappointing him. There were clear wins and losses, not subject to the whims of taste or committees; as he put it, chess was "logical and mechanistic."

Some Duchamp scholars see his chess playing and his art as intimately linked. The way chess pieces move through space and time, they say, reflects Duchamp's fascination with motion since *Nude*. Francis Naumann has argued that Duchamp's entire art career "resembles the move-by-move sequence of a chess game." Duchamp said, "Chess in itself is a hobby, is a game, everybody can play chess. But I took it very seriously and enjoyed it because I found some common points between chess and painting. Actually when you play a game of chess it is like designing something or constructing a mechanism of some kind by which you win or lose." He also noted that "it is important to remember that the pieces are merely physical markers for a contest that is principally mental." That is, in chess the board and pieces are representations of actions happening *entirely in the minds of the players*. That's the kind of art Duchamp always said he was trying to make.

One night he and Man Ray left the chess club around 1 a.m. and went uptown to Duchamp's space. In *Self Portrait*, Man Ray noted that Duchamp "worked at night when all was quiet and he wouldn't be disturbed." He described the Lincoln Arcade as

> a commercial loft building full of little enterprises:
> printers, tire vulcanizers, and nondescript shops.
> We climbed the stairway to his floor, walked
> through winding corridors until he stopped at a

door and opened it . . . [T]he interior presented
the same abandoned aspect as his first place;
nothing suggested a painter's studio. It was quite
large; there were steam radiators, and it was very
warm. In the middle of the floor stood a naked
bathtub with pipes running along the floor to the
sink plumbing against the wall. The floor was
littered with crumpled newspapers and rubbish . . .
in the far corner near the window stood a pair of
trestles on which lay a large piece of heavy glass
covered with intricate patterns laid out in fine lead
wires . . . A single unshaded bulb hung from the
ceiling to furnish the only light . . . Duchamp lit
his pipe and sat down in front of the glass. One
section of it bore an irregular mirrored surface
seen from the back, on which a delicate series of
ovals had been traced. With a razor blade he began
scraping at the unwanted silver. It was tedious
work; after a while he paused, put his hand over his
eyes and sighed: if he could only find a Chinaman
to perform this drudgery. I supposed he meant
a slavey.

The casual racism notwithstanding, this is a priceless
description of Duchamp at work—and not doing the
work. Decades later he'd say, "It bored me stiff. It

interested me, but not enough to be eager to finish it. I didn't care." When you view *Bride* today, you can actually see him losing interest in it. The images seem just to peter out.

Man Ray returned with a camera a few days later to shoot the glass panel with the dust on it. "Looking down on the work as I focused the camera, it appeared like some strange landscape from a bird's-eye view. There was dust on the work and bits of tissue and cotton wadding that have been used to clean up the finished parts, adding to the mystery. This I thought was indeed the domain of Duchamp." It's an eerie photograph. It looks like an abandoned Moon colony. Duchamp gave it the title *Élevage de poussière*, commonly translated as *Dust Breeding*.

·

That year Man Ray assisted in the creation of Duchamp's famous female alter ego, Rose Sélavy—soon to be spelled Rrose Sélavy, which when spoken with a French accent sounds like *Eros, c'est la vie*, another example of Duchamp's lifelong habit of putting an erotic spin on his work, especially when he could do it with puns and wordplay. Man Ray took Rrose's portrait in makeup and a fur wrap, making a rather unsuccessful try at looking seductively into the camera. Another portrait by Man Ray is even less convincing; Duchamp, gazing at us from under a ridiculous hat, just looks like a failed cross-dresser.

Asked why he invented Rose/Rrose, Duchamp said it wasn't to change his identity but to have two. We can certainly see her as another means of escape for him. Whereas R. Mutt—if he was, in fact, Duchamp's creation—was a one-off, he would use Rose/Rrose as his pseudonym and stand-in on all sorts of projects over the years. One of the first was a readymade that has led to the kind of ingenious conspiracy theorizing Duchamp's enigmatic work and ideas, probably more than any other artist of his time, inspire among his obsessive fans.

Duchamp enthusiasts—including the evolutionary biologist and New Yorker Stephen Jay Gould, who late in his life became fascinated with Duchamp—have argued that the 1921 readymade *Belle Haleine* (Nice Breath), which incorporated one of Man Ray's portraits of Rrose, was a veiled dig at one of the more intriguing figures in New York at the time, a powerhouse who went by the name Belle da Costa Greene. She was born into a prominent African-American household in Washington, D.C., in either 1883 (her version) or 1879. Her father, Richard Greener, was the first black graduate of Harvard and dean of the Howard University School of Law. When her parents separated, the light-skinned Belle, her mother, and sisters all started passing as white. She changed her surname to Greene to distance herself from her famous black father, and added da Costa so that she could claim to be of Portuguese heritage.

She was working at the Princeton University Library when she met the sixty-four-year-old J. P. Morgan, who immediately took a liking to her and hired her to be his private librarian. She was soon his confidant, adviser, and, it was widely rumored, one of his several mistresses. When asked about this later, she laughed and said, "We tried." She was well known for having plenty of other men. She ran the library long after Morgan's death in 1913, retiring in 1948 and dying two years later. Whispers had always circulated about her race—a society matron once sniffed that she was a "half-breed"—without ever quite landing.

Duchamp encountered Belle Greene shortly after arriving in New York in 1915. To cover his expenses, including his $40 a month rent at the Lincoln Arcade, he started giving private French lessons, like the ones for the Stetties, but tutoring wasn't paying enough. Considering his experience, he thought a library job would be good. He lobbied Walter Pach and John Quinn, who got him an interview with Greene, who got him a part-time job translating at the French Institute. He started in November 1915. She fired him six weeks later. Given how rudimentary his English was at the time, he no doubt made a lousy translator. But researcher Bonnie Green Garner, writing in *toutfait*, reported that Duchamp had been rather pleased with his job performance and must have been stunned and humiliated, again, by his dismissal.

Gould, Garner, and others have speculated that Duchamp may have gotten excruciatingly subtle revenge with his *Belle Haleine*. It started out as a bottle of the popular French perfume *Un air Embaumé* (Perfumed Air), created in 1914 by Rigaud. Duchamp washed away the bottle's original peach color and tinted it green—for Greene, they argue. He doctored the label's *Eau de Violette* (Violet Water), transposing two letters to read *Eau de Voilette* (Veil Water), and added *Belle Haleine*. He also added a Man Ray photo of himself as Rrose Sélavy (now with the two *r*s), wearing what Garner believed to be a very Belle Greene-ish outfit.

Was this peach-colored bottle in its green disguise an insinuating way of outing the secretly black woman who fired him? *Belle* plus the green plus the extra *r* in *Rrose* (for the *r* dropped off of *Greener*) plus the *Veil* plus the photo of him cross-dressing in her style . . .? Who knows. Duchamp enthusiasts love this sort of puzzle. What we know for certain is that in 2009 *Belle Haleine* fetched $11,500,000 in a Christie's auction, making it the most expensive Duchamp work ever sold.

•

Meanwhile, Katherine Dreier decided to start a modern art museum, and enlisted Duchamp's help. Duchamp brought along Man Ray, who came up with the name, Société Anonyme. He'd seen it in a French magazine and thought it meant "anonymous society." Duchamp laughed and explained it only meant an unincorporated business, but they stuck with it. It tickled them that when the papers were drawn up for the nonprofit, someone added "Inc." to the name, making it Unincorporated, Incorporated. Duchamp was president, Dreier the treasurer, Man Ray the secretary and official photographer. They rented an apartment in a brownstone at 19 East 47th Street, today the site of an office building that's home to the Ghana Consulate. Duchamp transformed the space into a boutique art museum with Duchampian flair. He put down rubber floors, covered the walls in blue oilskin, and, tongue firmly in cheek, created frilly lace-paper frames for all the paintings that hung there.

It had now been seven long years since the Armory show. The shock of the new art had worn off. Much more had come along since then to shock people, including the war, the 1918–19 Spanish Flu pandemic, which was deadlier than the war, and now Prohibition. Duchamp thought a light touch was in order. In a newspaper interview about the new museum (because of course he was the one the press turned to), he said, "People took modern art very seriously when it first reached America because they believed we took ourselves very seriously. A great deal of modern art is meant to be amusing." He suggested that if Americans exercised their "far-famed sense of humor," they'd enjoy the art more.

The Société Anonyme opened its doors for its first exhibition in April 1920. Despite the small space, they managed to show work by Van Gogh, Brâncuși, Jacques Villon, Joseph Stella, Morton Schamberg, Man Ray, and Duchamp himself. Henry McBride, the critic who'd previously written about Florine Stettheimer's *La Fête à Duchamp*, seemed to take Duchamp at his word about maintaining a sense of humor. With his high collars, owlish spectacles, and neat mustache, McBride looked every bit the priggish art snob. In fact, he was open-minded and sympathetic, and since the Armory Show he'd been the New York media's most enthusiastic booster for new art. He shared some of Duchamp's and Florine Stettheimer's puckish sense of humor. He once wrote privately to Florine that he thought Leo Stein was a "stuffed shirt." She painted two impish portraits of him. He and Duchamp came to like each other very much. It was to McBride that Duchamp declared how much he appreciated Louis Eilshemius's work in the Society of Independent Artists show in 1917.

McBride took reviewing the Société Anonyme's inaugural show for *The Sun and The New York Herald* newspaper as an occasion to satirize the stuffed shirts of the art establishment. He began by noting that the visitor must "mount two steep flights of stairs and then pay 25 cents" admission, but, he added, "Many a movie at twice the price gives one less to remember." He declared the assembled to be "some of the most willful, eccentric, daring, amusing, irreverent and powerful artists of the new schools . . . The pictures are not the kind that Academicians permit their wives and daughters to see."

McBride devoted most of his attention to Duchamp's entry. It was the piece Duchamp had created in Buenos Aires, two small glass panels in a metal frame, a study for *The Bride Stripped Bare*. It had to be the oddest "painting" McBride or anyone else had ever seen, but he treated it with admirable aplomb. The glass panels contained a precisely etched pyramid and circular shapes, with a magnifying glass glued to the surface of one panel, and a metal bar running through at a visually upsetting angle bearing its title in French, which translates as *To Be Looked at (from the Other Side of the Glass) with One Eye, Close to, for Almost an Hour*. In one way it was a Duchamp experiment in making the viewer part of the art: anyone who stood there with one eye shut and the other up close, staring through the piece for any length of time, would become more of a spectacle than the small and mostly transparent work itself. "Academicians will loathe M. Duchamp's work, and rightly, for M. Duchamp's art disturbs good persons who are almost at the point of buying," McBride joked. He added, "Academicians must not allow themselves to admire the workmanship—Academicians must not admire anything . . ."

Anticipating *The Bride Stripped Bare*, the glass in *To Be Looked at* was shattered when it was shipped from Argentina to New York. There was nothing to do but show it that way. It looked, McBride said, "as though the artist in the fury of composition had hauled off and struck the reluctant material a smashing blow with his hammer. M. Duchamp is really too daring."

Two years later, the Société published an intentionally ramshackle-looking book Duchamp put together, *Some French Moderns Says McBride*. It was a collection of McBride's *Sun and Herald* articles from 1915 to '21, with postcard-sized photo inserts, collected in a three-ring binder, with tabs. It looks like a high-schooler's notebook. As you go through it the typeface gets larger and larger on each page.

With Duchamp advising Dreier, often at a distance, the Société went on to mount eighty-five shows over twenty years, even in the face of stiff competition from

the new, better-funded Museum of Modern Art starting
in 1929. Kandinsky, Paul Klee, Alexander Archipenko,
and Léger had their first solo shows in America at
the Société.

•

When the exhibition closed in May 1920, Duchamp sailed
for Paris. Man Ray, still very much in his thrall, followed
in 1921. Duchamp met him at the station, found him
a cheap hotel room, and introduced him to the Dada
crowd, who in 1920 were enjoying their brief ascension
as the hippest art scene in Paris. Man Ray, the boy from
Brooklyn, was enchanted. Parisians called the 1920s *les
années folles*, the crazy years. Paris had quickly snatched
back its crown as the art capital of the West. Paris in the
1920s was hedonist and cosmopolitan and avant-garde and
wide open in ways that Prohibition New York, no matter
how flagrantly it flouted Prohibition, couldn't match. Paris
was an international free zone for sex in any flavor, liquor
that didn't come from a gangster's bathtub, drugs of all
kinds, and the leading edge of every art form. And given a
marvelously favorable exchange rate of the postwar franc
to the dollar, for Americans all the decadence and freedom
came exceedingly cheap. Americans of an arty or naughty
persuasion flocked there. "The whole of Greenwich

Village is walking up and down Montparnasse," Duchamp wrote the Stetties. Man Ray loved it so much he would not return to the States until World War II forced him to.

Duchamp, meanwhile, went back to Manhattan and stayed until 1923. When he next sailed for France that February, there was a sense of finality in it. "Except for three relatively brief trips to the United States in 1926–27, 1933–34, and 1936, he would live in France for the next twenty years," Calvin Tomkins reports. What he was running from this time is not quite clear, but one can take a guess. Before he sailed he left *The Bride Stripped Bare* in Dreier's hands. He had grown too bored with it to continue working on it and declared it "definitively unfinished." The magnum opus he had done all that thinking and planning about, put all that painstaking labor into, abandoned. He was thirty-five and seemed to have hit a creative brick wall. He was boring himself, a terrible thing for a person as creative as he was. Maybe he was hoping he'd find a new spark in France. In Paris he took a room in the same cheap hotel Man Ray was in.

For the next two decades, when anyone asked what he was up to—and they did, all the time—he declared that he was through with art and was focusing on his goal of becoming a chess champion instead. He spent a tremendous amount of time leaning over chessboards puffing a pipe, fostering the legend, which endures to this day, of Marcel Duchamp, the renegade anti-artist who had rejected art and now just played chess.

But for all the chess he played, and although he still wasn't painting paintings, he was hardly uninvolved in artistic matters. He was just involved in his own ways.

For one thing, he played a giant role in transforming the New York socialite Peggy Guggenheim into an influential gallery owner and one of the premier collectors and promoters of modern art in her time. Born in 1898, Guggenheim grew up, like the Stetties, in a prominent Jewish milieu in uptown Manhattan, taking annual grand tours of Europe. Her father, Benjamin, died on the *Titanic* in 1912; according to a survivor, he gave up his place in a lifeboat and dressed in evening clothes to meet his death with a gentleman's aplomb. However, he had left his business affairs in a mess, and when Peggy came into her inheritance, it was more modest than other people thought. She lived a rambunctious high life anyway. Carousing in Paris in the 1920s, she met Duchamp, Man Ray, Brâncuşi, Jean Cocteau, among others. "Marcel was a handsome Norman and looked like a crusader," she wrote in her 1946 memoir, *Out of This Century*. "Every woman in Paris wanted to sleep with him." So did she, but she was another of the women he sexually rebuffed.

Living in London in the 1930s, approaching forty, between men as she often was—she had just spent a year

being "entirely obsessed . . . by the strange creature,
Samuel Beckett"—and floundering for a purpose in life
(as she also often was), she decided to open an art gallery.
She knew little about art. "Marcel tried to educate me.
I don't know what I would have done without him.
To begin with, he taught me the difference between
Abstract and Surrealist art. Then he introduced me to all
the artists. They all adored him, and I was well received
wherever I went. He planned shows for me and gave me
lots of advice. I have him to thank for my introduction to
the modern art world."

Guggenheim Jeune—"a self-conscious echo of the
well-known Bernheim-Jeune gallery in Paris," Tomkins
explains—opened in Mayfair in January 1938 with a big
show by Jean Cocteau. Duchamp flew to London to hang
it. Although it was in operation only until June 1939,
the gallery showed work by Piet Mondrian, Kandinsky,
Yves Tanguy, and other moderns Duchamp had helped
Guggenheim select. Their very fruitful collaborations
would continue for years.

In a minor way Duchamp also got into movies. In
1924 he and Man Ray played chess on a rooftop in René
Clair's short film *Entr'acte*, made to be shown during the
intermission of a Dada ballet. Picabia, Erik Satie, and a
row of dolls with deflating balloon heads also feature in
it. Two years later, he and Man Ray made their own short

film, *Anemic Cinema*. Mesmerizing Op-Artish swirls lull the viewer, intercut with rotating puns and wordplay, like *Esquivons les Ecchymoses des Esquimaux aux mots Exquis* (Let's dodge the ecchymoses [bruises] of the Eskimos with exquisite words). They credited the film to Rrose Sélavy. He did a live performance too, appearing onstage nude, except for a fake beard, as Adam being handed an apple by Eve in a silly sex farce organized by Clair called *Ciné Sketch*.

More surprisingly, Duchamp became a transatlantic art dealer, the main conduit and promoter for his friend Brâncuşi's sculpture in New York. He had the notion that he and Brâncuşi could both make a few dollars from it, and they did. It's very hard to reconcile this with his scathing denunciations of the money-grubbing art market, selling creativity "like soap or securities," leading to "a massive dilution, a lowering of taste into the mist of mediocrity." But as the art historian John Golding wrote, "his is a career that can only be understood in terms of paradox." Or to quote Emerson, "With consistency a great soul has simply nothing to do."

Meanwhile, despite his regular pose of utter indifference to the art world and art history and artists' reputations, Marcel Duchamp worked very hard, in his usually unusual way, to preserve Marcel Duchamp's legacy in the annals of twentieth-century art. The project was called *Boîte-en-valise* (Box in a suitcase), credited to both himself and Rrose. He started on it in the mid-1930s and was still working on it when he had to flee the Nazis and sail back to New York in 1942. It was a carrying case in which he placed miniature reproductions of sixty-eight of his works: little photographs of *Nude* and *The Bride* and so on; even a tiny, sculpted version of *Fountain*. It's been compared to a traveling salesman's samples kit and a portable puppet theater. In a scathing pan of a Duchamp exhibition at the Walker Art Center in 1995, the art historian Philip Larson sneered:

> the Dirty Old Man's *Box* is the most masturbatory project of the century . . . as disturbingly self-promotional as Duchamp himself. The year is 1941. The artist hasn't done much art for years. He's putzed around the last five—God, was this character a putzer—contriving this encyclopedic apologia. The obsessive sequencing midst crossed referencing, the agony to find unity in diversity, the urge to force continuity where there is frag-mentation, to hide contradiction within consis-tency, and, yes, the longing for public approval after years of getting the short end of the critical shaft, even the longing for his lost readymades. *It's all here*. His career, once so brilliantly programmed

for freedom, now has trapped him in a box smaller
than a carpet salesman's sample book.

A portable, miniaturized Marcel Duchamp museum,
Boîte-en-valise was created by Marcel Duchamp, curated
by Marcel Duchamp, and *sold* by Marcel Duchamp when
he was able to crank out multiples of it when he got back
to New York. He was nothing if not consistently incon-
sistent. The Italian Duchamp enthusiast Arturo Schwarz,
who compiled the massive tome *The Complete Works of
Marcel Duchamp*, argued that Duchamp was living Keats's
negative capability, the capacity of the creative person to
embrace the mystery and uncertainty of things in pursuit
of truth and beauty. He saw Duchamp's inconsistencies
as "an attempt constantly to deceive life." Duchamp said,
"I force myself into self-contradiction to avoid following
my taste."

The influential New York collectors and gallery
owners Harriet and Sidney Janis, who were friends of
Duchamp, had their own opinion. In a 1945 essay they
would declare, "Perhaps more than any other living artist
in this revolutionary period, Duchamp has departed from
all existing norms . . . Despite the prevailing idea that
Duchamp has abandoned art, the high spiritual plane
in which all of his activity is conducted converts every
product . . . into a work of art."

Duchamp returned to New York for his first visit at the end of 1926, bringing Brâncuşi sculptures with him to exhibit and sell. (He would do this again in 1933.) Fresh disappointment awaited him. From November 1926 into January 1927, the Brooklyn Museum hosted "An International Exhibition of Modern Art Assembled by the Société Anonyme." Duchamp had spent six months helping Dreier find and choose the works to be included, taking her around to artists' studios and galleries in Paris. Picasso declined to be visited, but plenty of other artists agreed. In the exhibition catalogue, Dreier thanked Duchamp for his "indefatigable energy." Duchamp sailed back to New York to help mount the show. With more than three hundred works by sixty artists, it was the largest display of international art in the US since the Armory Show. Stieglitz and Man Ray had work in it, and Stella and Georgia O'Keeffe, and Picabia, Duchamp's brother Raymond, Juan Gris, Klee, Brâncuşi, Archipenko, and Kandinsky. It was the first time works by Joan Miró, Mondrian, and El Lissitzky were seen in New York. Eilshemius was in the show as well.

In one of the museum's galleries, Duchamp supervised the installation of *The Bride Stripped Bare by Her Bachelors, Even*. It was the first time it was seen in public.

If he was hoping it would stir up the sort of furor *Nude* had in 1913, he was bitterly disabused. It's strange now to see how little fanfare accompanied the unveiling of what later came to be considered one of the most remarkable artworks of the twentieth century. Dreier doesn't even mention it in what she wrote for the exhibition—and neither did most of the press, which must have caused him some real chagrin. It was, and is, one of the most enigmatic works in modern art. Two large planes of glass, and seemingly trapped between them, like specimens on slides, figures that, like the nude in *Nude*, seem to be caught in some state of biomechanical transfiguration. The eponymous Bride, in the upper left corner, looks maybe like a mechanical wasp, hovering and threatening. Her Bachelors, huddled together below, look like pawns in her game. The arcane machinery near them is inscrutable. And what about what look like bullet holes up near the Bride?

It wasn't until 1934 that Duchamp would put out a kind of guide to the work, another box, this one of assorted notes and sketches that's known as the *Green Box*, produced by Rrose Sélavy in an edition of three hundred. It would not be translated into English until 1960. One note states:

*The Bride, at her base, is a reservoir of
love gasoline. (or timid power). This
timid-power, distributed to the motor with
quite feeble cylinders, in contact with the sparks
of her constant life (desire-magneto) explodes
and makes this virgin blossom who has
attained her desire.*

In their humorously erotic, Futurist, and poetic way, the notes actually do explicate the art. But for the viewer standing before the work—whether in 1926 in Brooklyn or today at the Philadelphia Museum of Art—gazing at and *through* it, without a guide to explain it, it's an unsolvable puzzle. It "stands in relation to painting as *Finnegans Wake* does to literature," Tomkins writes, "isolated and inimitable; it has been called everything from a masterpiece to a tremendous hoax, and to this day there are no standards by which it can be judged." Peter Schjeldahl wrote, in a kind of shrug-in-print, "In my experience, it is more to be gawked at than quite relished, but it remains epically unusual."

At least Alfred Stieglitz seemed impressed by it. In a talk he gave at the museum, according to a notetaker in the audience, Stieglitz sat "on a raised platform beside the Duchamp glass, to which he pointed saying he considered it a privilege to sit beside it, and that it was one of the grandest works in the art of all time not excluding Egyptian, Chinese or even French, which was now the fad."

When the exhibition closed in January 1927, Dreier had *The Bride* crated and sent to a warehouse, where it sat, not commented on, for almost five years. Years later, Duchamp remained bitter about the piece's flat reception, saying, "it had no value in the artistic world at that time, nobody cared for it, nobody saw it or even knew about it." He ran right back to France that February.

Adding injury to insult, when Dreier visited him in Europe in 1931 she told him that *The Bride*'s two glass panels had been horribly shattered in shipment. Never one to surrender his poise in the presence of others, Duchamp merely shrugged when she told him. But when he made his trip back to the States in 1936 it was specifically to spend two months at Dreier's home, painstakingly piecing the work back together, shard by jagged shard. He then had it encased in two more layers of protective plate glass, the way it's seen today. He said he came to like the lightning-like webs of cracks that run through both panels, and one can see why. They add undeniable drama to it, a kind of tragic and kinetic grandeur. They complete it. They seem inevitable. As John Golding put it, with these fractures "the work has acquired the character of some giant icon, battered and venerable before its time."

In another display of apparent indifference to the art world, Duchamp sailed back to Paris that September. Had he waited until December, he could have seen eleven of his works included in the vast, groundbreaking group exhibition *Fantastic Art, Dada, Surrealism* at the Museum of Modern Art. Casting a wide net, the curator Alfred H. Barr Jr. included works by Hieronymus Bosch, Pieter Bruegel the Elder, Hans Holbein, and Leonardo da Vinci, along with Duchamp, Breton, Picasso, and other moderns. Situating the modern renegades of Dada and Surrealism in an art-historical context with old masters was a radical decision and an equal opportunity offender. Both believers in the classics and fans of the new thought that putting the two together was insulting. Katherine Dreier, who had loaned some of her Dada and Surrealist works to the show, took them away in a huff. Had he stayed around, Duchamp might have enjoyed the fireworks.

5 Back to the Future

*Had Marcel Duchamp not lived, it would have
been necessary for someone exactly like him
to live, to bring about, that is, the world
as we begin to know and experience it.*

*Duchamp's Glass is the first
x-ray-painting of space.*

Screwball Surrealist Marcel Duchamp

In August 1939 Peggy Guggenheim left London and
moved back to Paris. The German army wasn't far behind
her. She raced around the city in a frenzy, determined to
build a great private collection of modern art while there
was still time. "My motto was *Buy a picture a day,*" she
wrote, "and I lived up to it." She acquired voraciously.
The list is astounding: Salvador Dalí, Braque, Léger,
Picabia, Kandinsky, Klee, Magritte, Man Ray, Max Ernst,
Alberto Giacometti, Miró, Gris . . . It was like her own

personal Armory Show. With the Germans bearing down, artists were all in a panic to sell what they could and get out of Paris. Picasso was one of the rare few who denied her, kicking her out of his studio with a characteristically sexist snarl, "Lingerie is on the next floor."

In *Self Portrait* Man Ray writes evocatively about the arrival of the Germans, who rolled into Paris on June 14, 1940. He and everyone else who could get out, Duchamp and Guggenheim among them, flooded into the ostensibly free zone of southern France. Many crowded into the port of Marseilles, hoping for passage anywhere. Man Ray got out that year. Sailing into New York harbor, he writes, he was "overcome with a feeling of intense depression." He had reveled in his Paris life for twenty years and had done all his best work there. New York reminded him of his youthful failures. He soon left it for Hollywood, where he would stay until he moved back to Paris in 1951.

Guggenheim used her money and her American passport to get passage to New York for herself and her new lover, the painter Max Ernst, in the summer of 1941. She also managed to smuggle her new art collection to New York before the Nazis could get hold of it and condemn it all as "degenerate."

It took Duchamp until the following summer, June 1942, to reach New York, after arranging to ship the supplies to make fifty *Boxes*, which he was counting on for income. He was about to turn fifty-five. Unlike Man Ray, he was delighted to be back. And why not? While Paris would be a Nazi-infested ghost town until the end of the war, wartime New York was a boomtown, starting a climb that would take it to the apex of its twentieth-century trajectory. From the postwar years into the '60s, no city on the planet rivaled it for wealth, influence, or prestige. Among other factors, with Paris shut down, New York took over again as the art capital of the West and held that crown much longer this time than it had earlier in the century. Along with Duchamp and Ernst, the cream of European creative and intellectual life had fled the Nazis for New York. Their collective impact on New York's culture was going to be incalculable. Fulfilling what Duchamp had said to the press back in 1915, the ruins of Europe were the past, New York was the future.

Even though he was still insisting he wasn't an artist anymore, Duchamp was right where he needed to be. He'd make vacation trips to Europe, but Manhattan was now his permanent home for the rest of his life. He would become a naturalized citizen in 1955. In New York, during the last decades of his life, Duchamp's legend as the visionary who dynamited the old definitions of art would bloom, and he helped it along, the slightly aloof éminence grise of his own legacy.

When Peggy Guggenheim returned to the city, she
decided she wanted a museum/gallery of her own to rival
MoMA, which was hosting a big Picasso show at the
time, as well as her uncle Solomon's Museum of Non-
Objective Painting, which would become the Guggenheim Museum. While she and Max Ernst were scouting
locations, they saw a handsome town house at the end
of East 51st Street in Beekman Place with panoramic
views of the East River below. It was known as Hale
House because it was thought to be the site where the
British held the spy Nathan Hale before marching him
uptown to be hanged in 1776. (It wasn't. That was a block
away.) Instead of putting a museum there, they moved
in themselves. When Duchamp arrived in the summer of
1942 they invited him to stay with them. Between Ernst,
Peggy, and Peggy's two sons, who were as randy as she
was, Hale House was a scene of constant partying and
debauchery. Everybody who was anybody in arty New
York rolled in and stumbled out, from all the European
refugees to homegrown artists and writers like Carl
Van Vechten, Gypsy Rose Lee, Truman Capote, Djuna
Barnes, Joseph Cornell, Robert Motherwell, and Jackson
Pollock. "It was the coolest place in New York," Guggenheim declares in her book. Avant-garde composer John

Cage said that "in one fell swoop or series of evenings at Peggy Guggenheim's you met an entire world of both American and European artists . . . It was absolutely astonishing to be in that company."

Ernst had met the twenty-nine-year-old Cage and his wife, Xenia, in Chicago, and invited them to come to New York and stay at Hale House. Cage met Duchamp there at a party one night that summer. Tomkins relates that in return for room and board, Guggenheim wanted Cage to give a concert when she opened her museum, which she was planning for that fall. When she heard he was going to give one at her rival MoMA first, she flew into a rage and told the Cages to get out.

> Stunned by this harsh news—he was literally penniless at the time—Cage retreated through the usual crowd of revelers until he came to a room that he thought was empty, where he broke down in tears. Someone else was there, though, sitting in a rocker and smoking a cigar. "It was Duchamp," Cage said. "He was by himself, and somehow his presence made me feel calmer." Although Cage could not recall what Duchamp said to him, he thought it had something to do with not depending on the Peggy Guggenheims of this world.

Like Edgard Varèse but even more so, Cage was going to do for modern music what Duchamp had done for modern art. The son of an eccentric inventor in Los Angeles, an inveterate tinkerer himself, Cage used found sounds, manipulated objects, chance, and, famously, even silence to create what were in effect musical readymades. He guided listeners and students to reconsider all their traditional ideas about what was and wasn't music, the way Duchamp had done for the visual arts. The painter Alfred Leslie remembered a Cage lecture he attended in the Village.

It was the summer, with the window open on the street. He stood behind the lectern there, and he paused, and he took out a watch, and he put his watch down on the table, and just folded his arms and looked out and didn't say a word. And then he looked down and said, "One minute has passed. Any questions?" Of course he was pointing out that you had an opportunity here, the window being open, you heard all the sounds, the music, the composition that he had just created.

The courses Cage taught at the New School had a big impact on avant-garde New York in the 1950s and '60s, including the Fluxus group, of which Yoko Ono was a member, and Happenings, which he helped to invent.

Cage never failed to credit Duchamp as his major source of inspiration. "The effect for me of Duchamp's work was to so change my way of seeing that I became in my way a Duchamp unto myself," he said in an interview with Moira Roth. "Had Marcel Duchamp not lived, it would have been necessary for someone exactly like him to live, to bring about, that is, the world as we begin to know and experience it."

Yet for two decades he would be shy around the older man and very respectful of his privacy. "I didn't want to bother him with my friendship . . . I stayed away from him, out of admiration," he told Roth. He finally used chess as his way in. "[D]uring the winter holidays of '65–'66, the Duchamps and I were often invited to the same parties. At one of these I marched up to Teeny Duchamp [Duchamp's wife] and asked her whether she thought Marcel would consider teaching me chess. She said she thought he would." He met with them once or twice a week from then until Duchamp died in 1968. Because the chess was just an excuse, Cage never got any good at it. Duchamp "played so well and I played so poorly. So I played with Teeny, who also played much better than I. Marcel would glance at our game every now and then, and in between take a nap. He would say how stupid we both were. Every now and then he would get very impatient with me. He complained that I didn't seem to want to win. Actually, I was so delighted to be with him that the notion of winning was beside the point."

•

Peggy Guggenheim found a space for her museum/gallery, the top floor of a seven-story office building at 30 West 57th Street, in the midtown arts district that included her uncle's museum on East 54th, MoMA on West 53rd, and a number of galleries. She hired Frederick J. Kiesler, one of the most visionary architects of the time, to design it. Kiesler had known Duchamp in Paris in the 1920s, before he and his wife Stefi moved to Manhattan in 1926. He was soon commissioned to design New York City's first theater dedicated solely to film—no vaudeville entr'actes, no stage curtains or proscenium arch. His revolutionary Film Guild Cinema opened in 1929 on West 8th Street in Greenwich Village.

Kiesler admired Duchamp as a fellow Futurist. He wrote the first serious essay in English on *The Bride Stripped Bare*, published in the May 1937 issue of *Architectural Record*. At that point *Bride*, aka *Large Glass*, was still barely known in art circles. Kiesler traveled to Katherine Dreier's home in Connecticut to see it, bringing the great photographer Berenice Abbott along to take pictures. His article begins:

Architecture is control of space.
An Easel-Painting is illusion of Space-Reality.
Duchamp's *Glass* is the first x-ray-painting of
space.

"It surpasses in creative ingenuity any painting
since the great Illusion-Builder SEURAT," he went
on, "anticipating as well as continuing the line of
development Picasso-Miro-Dalí, X., Y., Z . . . It is
architecture, sculpture, and painting in one."

Kiesler was staunchly convinced of his own brilliance,
but his ideas were so far out of or ahead of his time that
he always struggled to get others to see it. He was quite
a handful for Guggenheim. "He was a little man about
five feet tall with a Napoleon complex. He was an unrec-
ognized genius, and I gave him a chance . . . to create
something really sensational. He told me that I would
not be known to posterity for my collection of paintings,
but for the way he presented them to the world in his
revolutionary setting."
True to his word, he designed a space that competed
with the art it was supposed to show. Art of This
Century, as Guggenheim named it, opened in October
1942. A reviewer in *Time* magazine described it as

a kind of artistic Coney Island. Here are shadow
boxes, peepholes, in one of which, by raising a
handle, is revealed a brilliantly lighted canvas
by Swiss painter Paul Klee. Another peep show,
manipulated by turning a huge ship's wheel, shows
a rotating exhibit of reproductions of all the works,
including a miniature toilet for MEN, by screwball Surrealist Marcel Duchamp. Beyond these
gadgets mankind swarms into what seems to be a
decorated subway. There spectators gaze at large
canvases by England's Leonora Carrington, Spain's
Joan Miró, Chile's Roberto Matta, all their works
unframed, suspended in the air from wooden arms
protruding from concave plywood walls. Every
two minutes, while onlookers enjoy the spectacle,
a roar as of an approaching train is heard, lights go
out on one side of the gallery, pop on at the other.

Because Duchamp had guided Guggenheim's collect-
ing, Art of This Century was heavy on Dada and Surrealism. But it also showcased young New York artists, who
were in the process of inventing a new genre of their own
that the *New Yorker* would label Abstract Expressionism,
America's first truly homegrown avant-garde. Duchamp
didn't care much for it—it was just more "retinal" art to
him—but as Guggenheim's adviser he helped her pick

and nurture the best of them, including Jackson Pollock, Mark Rothko, Robert Motherwell, and Clyfford Still, who all had their first solo shows there. Duchamp also suggested a show of only female artists and, with Ernst and Breton, was on the jury who selected a remarkable group of thirty-one artists, including Frida Kahlo, Meret Oppenheim, Leonora Carrington, Louise Nevelson, Dorothea Tanning (who ran off with Ernst), Gypsy Rose Lee, and the late Baroness Elsa.

The exhibition at Art of This Century in December of 1942 paired Duchamp's *Box* with some of Joseph Cornell's boxes. They had met in 1933 during one of Duchamp's rare trips back to New York in that period, at a Brâncuşi exhibition that Duchamp had helped organize. Then, one afternoon in the summer of 1942, Duchamp answered the phone at Hale House, no one else being around. The caller was Cornell, who was shocked to hear Duchamp's voice. He wrote in his diary that it was "one of the most delightful and strangest experiences I ever had." He worked up the nerve to invite Duchamp to visit him in Flushing, and Duchamp, who surely had never been to Queens before, did. Getting Marcel Duchamp, the dark prince of the avant-garde, to come out to Flushing was a coup of some magnitude. They remained friends and great admirers of each other for the rest of Duchamp's life.

"What an unlikely pair," the curator and art historian Anne d'Harnoncourt wrote decades later, "the charming, ironic, profoundly sophisticated Frenchman, whose acquaintance with the art world on both sides of the Atlantic was encyclopedic . . . and the shy, reclusive American . . ." Yet, she added, they were both "in search of the marvelous" and both "[a]t heart *bricoleurs*, scribblers, and tinkerers . . . absorbed in making fresh magic out of the vast plethora of things around them."

Cornell lived most of his life with his aging mother and disabled brother in the house at 37–08 Utopia Parkway in Flushing, Queens. Still standing in 2025, the Cornell home is a small, wood-framed house on a block of similar houses in a neighborhood that's almost but not quite middle class and almost but not quite suburban. The California curator and gallerist Walter Hopps, who played significant roles in promoting both Duchamp and Cornell, met Cornell there in 1959. He described "a two-story, gabled Yankee house with a sizable attic and an enclosed porch . . . It was full of things—very neat, but stuffed to the point where it could make some people nervous. Cornell was quiet and serious; for him to smile was a rare event, so you really noticed it when he did. At times he seemed almost otherworldly."

Since making boxes was what Cornell did, Duchamp hired him for a while to help him crank out multiples of

Boîte-en-valise. Duchamp loved Cornell's own boxes, had some, and showed them off when people visited. Like Florine Stettheimer and Eilshemius, Cornell was an original, an eccentric, almost but not really an Outsider. For his part, Cornell idolized Duchamp and, obsessive collector of nostalgic ephemera that he was, he filled a box with Duchampian memorabilia. Found among the many, many things he left in his home when he died in 1972, it is called the "Duchamp Dossier." According to the Philadelphia Museum of Art, where it resides, it contains "typed and handwritten notes, letters, and postcards, Photostats, paper, newspaper and magazine clippings, exhibition announcements, printed papers, printed reproductions, and drawings, objects, and ready-mades by Duchamp and Cornell."

After a groundbreaking run of exhibitions, Guggenheim closed Art of This Century in 1947 and moved to Venice, where she made her Palazzo Venier dei Leoni in the Dorsoduro the art magnet it still is.

•

A week before Art of This Century opened in October 1942, an exhibition organized by André Breton called *First Papers of Surrealism* opened in the Whitelaw Reid mansion at 451 Madison Avenue between East 50th and

51st Streets. At the time, it was serving as the elegant headquarters for French war relief efforts. It was later incorporated into Harry Helmsley's Palace Hotel. "First Papers" was a term from immigration applications, and the forty artists in the show included Ernst, René Magritte, Tanguy, and other European refugees, but not the most famous Surrealist of the era, Dalí, whose ceaseless self-promotion and love of money had put him out of favor with other Surrealists. They called him Avida Dollars. Also in the show was the young American Robert Motherwell, who had arrived in New York a couple of years earlier. This was important early exposure for his work. Although he would develop into a leading Abstract Expressionist, Motherwell had a deep interest in and respect for Dada and Surrealism that the Ab-Exers didn't all share. The artist Barnett Newman would feud with him about it, and the critic Clement Greenberg, great champion of Ab-Ex, would go positively apoplectic over it. Motherwell was particularly admiring of and friendly with Duchamp.

The October 26, 1942, *Newsweek*, an issue dominated by war news, ran a review titled "Agonized Humor." It called the exhibition the "biggest all-surrealist show ever seen in the United States." It went on, stumbling over a few errors:

The two ringmasters who arranged it are André
Breton, the group's leader and theoretician, and
Marcel Duchamp, whose famous "Nude Descending the Staircase" [*sic*] was part of the Armory
Show of 1913 that helped shock America into a
consciousness of modern art. Duchamp hasn't
painted in twenty years; he spends most of his
time playing chess and writing books about it.
But he made the show's chef d'oeuvre: a fantastic
labyrinth in the main exhibition room woven
from 16 miles of string and intertwined with the
crystal chandeliers. It was intended to "combat the
background," which it does effectively.

Breton had asked Duchamp to dress up the mansion's formal Gilded Age rooms into something more
appropriate for a Surrealist exhibit. With a meagre
budget, Duchamp used twine to fill the space with a
giant spiderweb in which the artworks hung like trapped
insects, some barely visible. As usual, not everyone got
or liked Duchamp's humor. To the complaints that it
made the work hard to see, he shrugged, saying, "You
can always see through if you want to." Another classic
Duchampianism.

•

The same month, Duchamp moved out of Hale House
and rented a room and bath in the Kieslers' penthouse
apartment in the upwardly tumbling traffic-sooted pile
of brick that is the Candela Tower apartment building at
56 7th Avenue and West 14th Street. It was not any quieter
than Hale House had been. The Kieslers liked partying as
much as the Guggenheim clan did, and the same hip, arty
crowd who packed Hale House crammed into the elevator
up to their place. Duchamp loved it because it was near
the Marshall Chess Club, which in 1931 had moved
into what's still its home, the handsome town house at
23 West 10th Street, between 5th and 6th Avenues.

He stayed with the Kieslers for a year. Then, in
October 1943, he moved around the corner to 210 West
14th Street between 7th and 8th Avenues, a five-story
town house known as the Pompeo Coppini Studio. The
block was a low-rent commercial strip spangled with
a few artists' lofts. A locally famous Spanish grocery,
Casa Moneo, was in the street level storefront at 210
for decades. As of 2025, the space housed a nail salon.
Coppini was an Italian sculptor who bought the house
in the 1920s, installed artists' studios on the top floor,
and placed a bas-relief of an artist at work over the front
door. This is sometimes misidentified as a "portrait of
Duchamp," though it predated his residency by years.
Duchamp rented two small rooms on the top floor and

walked up and down the four flights of stairs from 1943 to 1965.

He carried on with his ascetic life in one of the rooms. He once told an interviewer that "the life of an artist is like the life of a monk," then added with a sly grin, "a lewd monk." "It was a medium-sized room," a visitor recalled. "There was a table with a chessboard, one chair, and a packing crate on the other side to sit on, and I guess a bed of some kind in the corner. There was a pile of tobacco ashes on the table, where he used to clean his pipe. There were two nails in the wall, with a piece of string hanging down from one. And that was all." Another visitor opined: "It seems a strange place for a high-brow to live, but that is probably the very reason Duchamp has chosen it—to outwit anyone who might expect him to compromise his individuality by doing the obvious thing . . . His rent is \$40 a month, fitting into an extremely economical budget by means of which he succeeds in outwitting the whole competitive commercial rat race of New York." There were no cooking facilities. There were plenty of cheap eateries in the neighborhood.

Next to that room was a shared bathroom, with a locked door that opened to the tiny room that became his studio. He let almost no one into this second room, because it was where, probably in 1946, he began to work on a project he kept so secret only a few close friends would know about it until after he died. "He had two studios," John Cage explained to Moira Roth, "the one people knew about, and one next door to it, where he did his work, which no one knew about. That's why people were able to visit his studio and see nothing going on. As he expressed it later, it was a way of going underground."

Meanwhile, *The Bride Stripped Bare* got a new temporary home. In 1943 Katherine Dreier loaned it to MoMA, where, in all its fractured, mysterious glory, it got its first extended public exposure, on view there for more than two years. Duchamp oversaw the move.

If he really thought he was going to able to go underground, he was sorely mistaken. Quite the opposite was happening. In wartime and postwar New York, once again the art capital of the West, he was hailed as a celebrity more than ever before, embraced by the art world, the media, and society as a grand old (rascally, tricky) figure of the modern age. Tomkins wrote, "Without any apparent effort on his part, Duchamp hovered like a benign genie over the New York art scene." In a letter to Dreier, Duchamp wrote, "I am dumbfounded at my position as a kind of 'vedette' [star, idol] in this town," adding the characteristically ironic, "and not to be able to at least make an ordinary living out of it."

View, an avant-garde New York magazine, devoted
its March 1945 issue to Duchamp. He designed the
cover, and he and Kiesler collaborated on a complex
six-page photomontage. It included a triptych centerfold
of *The Bride Stripped Bare*. The back cover image was a
Duchamp poem composed in a jumble of type: "Quand /
la fumée de tabac / sent aussi / de la bouche / qui l'exhale,
/ les deux odeurs / s'épousent par / infra-mince" (When
the tobacco smoke also smells of the mouth that exhales
it, the two odors marry by infra-thin.) *Infra-thin* was one
of Duchamp's pseudo-scientific neologisms describing
the slight trace or impact of one object on another, like
the lingering warmth on a seat when you stand up, or,
as in this case, the effect of the smoke and the mouth on
each other. Kiesler, Breton, and others wrote euphoric
praise of Duchamp. It was, according to Duchamp
curator and scholar Michael R. Taylor, "the most ambi-
tious, elaborate, and expensive number" in the magazine's
seven-year run.

That July, on the cover of *Vogue* was a fashion model
photographed through the cracked glass of *The Bride
Stripped Bare* in a shoot at MoMA. At the end of the year,
MoMA bought from Walter Pach *The Passage from the
Virgin to the Bride*, which Duchamp painted in Munich
in 1912. Duchamp had given it to Pach in thanks for his
friendship and support in 1915. It wasn't MoMA's first

Duchamp. The museum had acquired his short film *Anemic Cinema* in 1938. But *Passage* could be said to be the MoMA's first major Duchamp.

The Dada Painters and Poets, an anthology edited by Robert Motherwell—with much help from Duchamp and others—was published in New York in 1951. It was another step toward Duchamp's art world canonization/demonization. Some of Motherwell's fellow Abstract Expressionists were not pleased. They were sorely aware that Duchamp had denigrated art that was purely retinal and gestural, which pretty well described Abstract Expressionism. According to Tomkins, Duchamp called the movement a "debacle in painting," and once suggested, when Guggenheim was having trouble fitting Pollock's 20-foot-long *Mural* into a space, that she cut some off one end, since no one would notice.

"Marcel Duchamp tried to destroy art by pointing to the fountain, and we now have museums that show screwdrivers and automobiles and paintings," Barnett Newman complained. Museums "have accepted this esthetic position that there's no way of knowing what is what . . . [I]f Motherwell wishes to make Marcel Duchamp a father, Duchamp is his father and not mine nor that of any American painter that I respect."

On cue, *Life* magazine ran its big "Dada's Daddy" article in its April 28, 1952, issue. "This month a rather strange assortment of people crowded into a small but elegant basement art gallery in Manhattan to view a rather strange assortment of painting and sculpture and to greet an equally strange artist who was responsible for the chief exhibit," it began. "The people include middle-aged critics, artists and directors of art museums who are capable of appreciating a fur-lined teacup as well as a Picasso." The "chief exhibit" was one of Duchamp's *Boîte-en-valise* multiples. The article was a surprisingly lengthy disquisition on the history and cultural significance of Dada, with pages of four-color reproductions of Duchamp's art and Eliot Elisofon's wonderful multiple-exposure *Nude*-like photograph of sixty-four-year-old Duchamp descending a staircase.

From *View* to the cover of *Vogue* to a big spread in *Life*: Duchamp hadn't seen so much press since he first arrived in New York in 1915. Despite insisting that he just wanted to be left alone to play chess, Duchamp cheerfully cooperated with and even collaborated on it all.

•

To his enduring credit, Duchamp remained as interested in promoting his friends' art and careers as his own. When his old friend Florine Stettheimer died in 1944, at seventy-two, he worried that her work, which she'd always hesitated to promote, might be forgotten. He wrote to MoMA, noting his "personal admiration for her work," and suggested that they host a posthumous retrospective. The exhibition, which he helped organize, opened in October 1946. It was her first solo show at a major institution, and the first solo show of any female artist in MoMA's history. It laid the groundwork for the appreciation her work enjoys today—all unlikely had Duchamp not made it happen.

Duchamp still had his own legacy to look after as well. In the late 1940s, out in Hollywood, the aging Arensbergs negotiated to leave their art collection to University of California Los Angeles (UCLA). According to Tomkins, it encompassed thirty-seven Duchamps, including almost all the important ones, plus Picassos, Braques, Brâncuşis, Klees, "and approximately eight hundred other works, many of the highest quality." When the UCLA deal fell through, museums around the country leapt: MoMA and The Metropolitan Museum in New York wooed the Arensbergs, as did the Art Institute of Chicago, Harvard, Stanford, the National Gallery, and others. The Arensbergs, ailing, enlisted Duchamp to do the negotiating and choosing for them. In 1950 he struck the deal. Much as he loved New York and had made it his hometown-away-from-home, the collection would not be going there, but to the Philadelphia Museum of

Art, which had outmaneuvered all competitors to win his favor. After Louise and Walter died within months of each other in 1953/4, Duchamp personally oversaw the installation of their Duchamps at the museum. Added to theirs was *The Bride Stripped Bare by Her Bachelors, Even*, which Katherine Dreier left to the museum upon her death in 1952. Duchamp supervised its installation as well. As Tomkins notes, his friends had left him in the enviable position of an artist with a direct hand in the disposition of his own heritage. The works went on display in 1954 and are still there today.

6 *Étant donnés*

*It is only fitting that Duchamp's last gift
to the world should be the apotheosis
of enigma, direct but infinitely mysterious.*

In 1946 Duchamp gave his current lover a small work
of art, an amorphous squiggle on a bit of acrylic film,
mounted on black satin, in a wooden frame. It had another
of his enigmatic titles, *Paysage fautif* (Faulty Landscape).
It's indicative of the intense level of curiosity and study
Duchamp's work inspires that in 1987 *Paysage fautif* was
sent to an FBI lab in Houston for chemical analysis to
determine what the amorphous squiggle was made of.

It was semen. Duchamp, approaching sixty, had
declared his love, or at least his lust, by jerking off and
giving the result to his lover. Framed. Inevitably, this has
been called a "seminal" work, a joke he could have come
up with himself.

It's likely that his lover, Maria Martins, knew what it
was. They had that kind of sex-charged relationship. It's

another of Duchamp's coups that it took the rest of the world more than forty years and an FBI investigation to figure it out.

He most likely had met the Brazilian Surrealist sculptor in 1943, at a 57th Street gallery's exhibition of her striking work in the two-artist show *Maria: New Sculptures* and *Mondrian: New Paintings*. She was married to the Brazilian ambassador to the US, dividing her time between D.C., where she was known to throw great parties, and New York, where evidently every hetero male on the art scene made a play for her. She chose Duchamp. Martins was his inspiration, his main model, and his first assistant for his secret 14th Street project *Étant donnés*, his last great—and greatly baffling—work of art. Their affair lasted into 1950, when she left New York, eventually to return to Brazil with her husband and children.

Soon enough she was replaced in Duchamp's life by Alexina Matisse. She was born in Cincinnati and went by the nickname Teeny all her life. In Paris in the early 1920s she studied sculpture under Brâncuşi, met Duchamp, and married the art dealer Pierre Matisse, son of Henri Matisse. They broke up in 1949 and in 1951 she was reintroduced to Duchamp by Max Ernst and Dorothea Tanning. When Ernst and Tanning moved to France, Teeny and Duchamp took over their fourth-floor walkup on East 58th Street. He kept 14th Street to work

on *Étant donnés*, taking the bus back and forth as though
to a job. In January 1954 he and Teeny took the subway
to City Hall and got married. She was forty-eight, he was
sixty-six. Unlike his abortive first marriage in France in
1927, this one stuck. Teeny took over as his model and
helper on *Étant donnés*. In 1959 they moved to Greenwich
Village, to the beautiful 1850s town house at 28 West
10th Street between 5th and 6th Avenues. At various times
Dashiell Hammett, Paul and Jane Bowles, and the theater
critic Mel Gussow lived there. A bonus for Duchamp
was that the Marshall Chess Club was (and is) across the
street. It would be his last address in New York City.

Duchamp clearly enjoyed his growing repute in his
final years, and he helped it along any way he could.
Interest in him heated up when the Arensberg collection
went on display at the Philadelphia Museum of Art in
October 1954. Other museums and galleries in various
cities followed suit, showing whatever collections of
Duchamp's works they could pull together. Books about
him in French and English began to flow, the start of a
coming flood. Not one but two large catalogues raisonnés
were published, Robert Lebel's *On Marcel Duchamp*, in
1959, and Arturo Schwarz's giant tome, *The Complete
Works of Marcel Duchamp*, a decade later. Duchamp had
a strong hand in what they said and how they looked,
still managing his legend without ever dropping his pose

of cool indifference to it. The first English translation of his *Green Box*, Richard Hamilton's *The Bride Stripped Bare by Her Bachelors, Even*, was published in 1960 and introduced an avid new generation to the occult mysteries of his thinking. There were interviews on television, newspaper and magazine articles, and many invitations to speak and to participate in learned panels.

In 1963 in Utica, New York, Duchamp was the guest of honor at an exhibition celebrating the fiftieth anniversary of the Armory Show; he quipped, "Having heard so much of the Amory Show, all my life, I am thrilled to at last see it . . ." That same year, Walter Hopps organized a career retrospective at the Pasadena Art Museum in California. It was a great success and has been credited with inspiring a generation of West Coast Pop and Conceptual artists, including Ed Ruscha, Edward Kienholz, and Bruce Nauman. It was also the setting for the famous photo shoot by Julian Wasser of Duchamp, nattily dressed as always, playing chess with naked, voluptuous twenty-year-old Eve Babitz. It was the photographer's idea. Babitz, who was seeing Hopps, said yes because she was feuding with him and wanted to make him jealous; Duchamp said yes because of course he did.

Andy Warhol had come from New York to Los Angeles for an exhibition of his own work and met up with Duchamp and Teeny at the museum. In 1966

Duchamp would sit for one of Andy's Screen Test films.
Not surprisingly, they were sympatico, as much as
Warhol could be sympatico with anyone. He considered
Duchamp a genius, though, like Duchamp, he also liked
to appear to keep his cool. He was especially impressed
by the concept of readymades. The debt his soup cans
and Brillo boxes owe to Duchamp is obvious. Duchamp
admired him in turn. "What's interesting is not that
somebody would want to paint 27 soup cans," he said.
"What's interesting is the mind that would conceive of
painting 27 soup cans." High praise from him. He also
said, "I like Warhol's spirit. He's not just some painter or
movie-maker. He's a filmeur, and I like that very much."

•

At the end of 1965, 210 West 14th Street was sold and
Duchamp had to find a new studio to continue his work
on *Étant donnés*. The piece had grown into a bizarre
diorama that filled the whole of the tiny studio. "He
carefully disassembled the intricate *tableau vivant* that
he had worked on for so many years and transported its
more fragile elements himself, making countless trips
down the four flights of stairs and then proceeding
by taxi to 80 East 11th Street, where he had rented a
small room," Calvin Tomkins wrote. The building at

80 East 11th Street was originally the St. Denis Hotel, built in 1853. Ulysses S. Grant, Mark Twain, Sarah Bernhardt, Buffalo Bill Cody, and P. T. Barnum had all stayed there in its glory days, which were well past by 1965. When Duchamp moved *Étant donnés* into Suite 403, the building had been downgraded to a bland office building, which would be razed in 2019 to make room for a much larger, equally bland new office building. "Duchamp spent the first two months of 1966 reassembling the work in this anonymous space, whose single window overlooked an air shaft," Tomkins reported.

Duchamp played another public game of chess in March 1968, in the Ryerson Theatre in Toronto. Not with a nude young woman this time but with John Cage. As annoyed as he often was with John Cage as a chess player, Duchamp did like his musical ideas, which after all were so very Duchampian. He also came to admire Cage's partner, the choreographer Merce Cunningham, for whom Cage had left Xenia, and their painter friends Robert Rauschenberg and Jasper Johns, all of whom mutually admired Duchamp. Johns's beer cans, bull's-eyes, and multiplied American flags all show obvious, unashamed debts to Duchamp. His sprawling, barely contained 1964 painting *According to What* is a flat-out homage to Duchamp, encrusted with found objects, with a wire jutting out in a direct reference to *Tu m'* and even a sneaky portrait of Duchamp in one corner. The gloriously messy spectacle might just as well be titled *According to Marcel*. Rauschenberg's equally unruly paintings and his "combines," like *Monogram*, the goat stuffed into a big tire, also owe a clear debt to Duchamp and readymades. He called Duchamp "a constant inspiration." Through these disciples, Moira Roth noted, Duchamp's ideas would "spread generally among artists involved in 'assemblage' and 'junk' sculpture and 'happenings.'"

Cage had conceived the public chess game as a performance, titled *Reunion*. The chessboard was wired with photo resistors that generated different sounds each time the players moved their pieces: as they played they were spontaneously composing completely aleatoric music. The event went awry when Duchamp quickly defeated Cage. Teeny agreed to play a second game with Cage, while Duchamp sat to one side puffing a cigar. A large audience had shown up to see the two avant-garde giants together on stage, but their numbers dwindled as the event dragged on from 8:30 in the evening to around 1 a.m. At that point only about ten spectators remained, one of whom called out, "Encore!"

A few nights later, Merce Cunningham and his dance company premiered a new piece, *Walkaround Time*, with a striking set by Jasper Johns that deconstructed and enlarged elements from *The Bride Stripped Bare*.

Duchamp and Teeny were there for it; Duchamp, looking delighted, joined the company for curtain calls. Later that month, a large exhibition, *Dada, Surrealism, and Their Heritage*, opened at MoMA. It included thirteen Duchamp works. He and Teeny were at the gala opening.

After that they left for a European idyll. They arrived in Paris just in time for the May 1968 massive student uprising that paralyzed the city. Duchamp disapproved of it, as he did all political activity. The studio that he had inherited from his sister was in the suburb of Neuilly, putting him and Teeny outside the chaos zone. On July 28 they met Man Ray and his wife Juliet in a little restaurant near the studio to celebrate Duchamp's eighty-first birthday. The birthday cake had "cigars around it instead of candles," Juliet later recalled.

On October 1 the Man Rays, Duchamp's friend and biographer Robert Lebel, and his wife, Nina, gathered for dinner with Duchamp and Teeny at the Neuilly studio. It was "pleasant and lots of red wine," Juliet remembered. "Marcel was in good spirits, talking and laughing . . . We left around 11:30." About 1 a.m., Duchamp "went into the bathroom to get ready for bed," Tomkins writes. "It seemed to Teeny that he was staying longer than usual. She called to him, but there was no answer. When she went in, he was lying on the floor, fully dressed." His heart had failed. "'He had the most calm, pleased expression on his face,' she said."

Of course he did. He had made his last and maybe greatest escape. When *Étant donnés*, his almost universally unexpected and arguably most provocative work, was unveiled to the public a year later, he did not for once have to deal with how anyone responded.

•

Teeny and her son Paul Matisse worked with a curator at the Philadelphia Museum of Art, Anne d'Harnoncourt, to disassemble *Étant donnés* in Suite 403 on East 11th Street, ship it, and reassemble it in the museum. Duchamp had left no notes explaining the meaning of the strange work, but he did write detailed instructions on how to install it. It has, unsurprisingly, never been moved since.

Just finding *Étant donnés* in the museum is a quest. You walk down one hallway past numerous art-filled galleries on your left and right, then turn and continue down a much longer hallway, past many more galleries filled with much more art, until, just as you begin to suspect you've been misdirected or maybe pranked— which, considering it's Duchamp you're searching for, is not entirely far-fetched—the Duchamp gallery winks at you through a doorway on your right.

Because of the Arensberg bequest, the museum holds the world's largest public collection of Duchamps. But what's on display is easily contained in one modest-sized room and two small alcoves. Most of the best-known pieces are there: *Nude Descending a Staircase, No. 2*, reproductions of *Fountain* and *Bicycle Wheel*, and of course *The Bride Stripped Bare by Her Bachelors, Even*, given pride of place in the room. It's not crowded. To his detractors, the scantness of objects in Duchamp's oeuvre is a significant fault. "Duchamp occupies a very special place in the history of modern art," the conservative critic Hilton Kramer argued. "No other artist in our century (or perhaps in any century) made so great an impact on artistic consciousness on the basis of so slender an accomplishment . . . [H]e is a minor artist, and very often a trivial one." But even Kramer felt compelled to note that with Duchamp, it's not the objects but the ideas that count: "Yet as an esthetic ideologue, as the promulgator of attitudes and ideas about art rather than as a maker of works of art, he was a major force . . ."

To find *Étant donnés* you must step into one of the two small alcoves. It's dimly lit and inherently mysterious. Stepping in there has been compared to entering a Catholic confession booth (Duchamp was a lapsed Catholic), an oracle's grotto, and a porn peepshow booth. At first all you see is an ancient, weathered wooden door set in an archway of bricks in the far wall. If you don't know what you're looking for, you won't see it. People have been known to step into the alcove, glance briefly at the old door, and just walk out, probably thinking they've made a wrong turn. You have to walk up to the door and notice its two peepholes in it.

No photo or description can prepare the first-time viewer for the visceral impact of what you see when you look through those magnifying peepholes. You're spying on a very strange, disturbing, erotic, comedic three-dimensional scene. Right before you, just beyond a broken stone wall, a life-sized naked woman lies spread-eagle on a bed of twigs and branches, thrusting her hairless sex at you. The pose is very reminiscent of Baroness Elsa. Her blond hair covers her face. In her left hand she holds up an antique-style gas lamp, lit. The scenery behind her, eerie or enchanted or both, is a wooded landscape under a sky the greenish hue of a bruise. In the distance is a waterfall, surely intentionally tacky, that glitters mechanically like the light-up moving pictures one sometimes sees in junk stores or behind the bar in old taverns. Like all of Duchamp's previous works, it's nothing like any of Duchamp's previous works. It is as rare and eccentric as can be. After the sort-of-Dada and near-Surrealism of all his previous work, the hyper-realism here is startling.

In the lavish 2009 *Marcel Duchamp: Étant donnés*,
Philadelphia Museum curator Michael R. Taylor detailed
what was known—given the secrecy of the project—
about how Duchamp constructed it over twenty years.
Duchamp even kept the secret from Arturo Schwarz,
whom he knew to be amassing his giant catalogue rai-
sonné, *The Complete Works of Marcel Duchamp*. The first
edition of the 630-page book (which has been revised and
expanded over the years to nearly 800 pages) was actually
at the printer in 1969 when Schwarz learned about *Étant
donnés* and had to make an emergency re-edit.

Probably in 1946, Maria Martins posed nude for a
sketch, more disturbing than erotic, of her torso, headless
and armless, with her legs splayed wide to show off
her vagina à la the Baroness. She joined Duchamp for
private lessons in plaster casting from an art instructor at
Columbia University. They then made a cast of her body
in that awkward spread-eagle pose, legs thrown wide.
Duchamp then spent much time experimenting with various processes for covering the mold with realistic-looking
skin, trying leather, pig skin, and parchment.

After Martins left and Teeny entered his life in the
1950s, she became his second model and assistant. He
cast her left arm for the figure. Eventually he hand-built
an armature, Taylor explains, using "steel, wire, wood,
commercial putty, adhesive, and cold 'solder,'" and

fastened the manikin to it "with countless small brass screws." All in his tiny garret studio on 14th Street, and all of it new to him, involving much frustrating trial and error. This, along with Duchamp's habit of working only in spurts, explains why it stretched into years and then a couple of decades.

He based the landscape and waterfall behind her on a place in Switzerland he had visited. The idea for hiding the scene behind a door probably came from a visit he and Teeny made in 1958 to the home of the psychoanalyst Jacques Lacan. Lacan had recently bought Gustave Courbet's equally shocking 1866 painting *The Origin of the World*, showing the nude torso of a woman, reclining, a sheet drawn back to expose her open legs, her hairy vagina in the foreground thrust into the viewer's gaze. Lacan, like all previous owners of the painting, hid it behind a wooden panel that he could slide open to show to the appropriate guest.

Teeny helped Duchamp search for the old door he used; they found it in Spain in the early 1960s and had it shipped over and brought up to the fifth floor at 14th Street. Putting the peepholes in the door is pure Duchamp. He didn't find the old bricks to frame the door until shortly before he died in 1968. He and Teeny gathered them from construction and demolition sites near the studio.

The title harkens back to *Green Box* and a note about *The Bride Stripped Bare*:

Étant donnés: 1° la chute d'eau / 2° le gaz d'éclairage

Which Richard Hamilton translated as

Given 1. the waterfall
         2. the illuminating gas

It seems the start of one of Duchamp's scientific-sounding propositions, but he left the viewer to complete it.

Duchamp enthusiasts have labored ever since to decipher what he intended to say with *Étant donnés*. Did he really go to all that work just to leave a last fuck-you toodle-oo to the world of art and art lovers? *Tu m'*, *toujours tu m'*? Was he equating art and pornography? Is *Étant donnés* an elaborate peepshow booth, making every viewer a voyeur? Is this the Bride finally not only stripped bare but splayed wide open in front of everyone who spies through those peepholes? Does that make us worse than her haplessly horny Bachelors, worse than voyeurs—eye-rapists?

•

When *Étant donnés* went on view in July 1969, the
world press flocked to that little alcove. So did the public.
A spokesperson for the museum said that the *Étant
donnés* was "packing them in" that July, responsible for
attendance numbers "double and sometimes triple the
normal for this time of year."

Jasper Johns called it "the strangest work of art any
museum has ever had in it." The Ab-Ex artist Cleve Gray,
writing in *Art in America*, called it "an erotic creche."
Brooks Adams wrote, "[O]ne enters this private 'chapel'
as a sort of pilgrim, but one exits a voyeur."

The *Village Voice* declared it "a masterpiece [that] calls
up for discussion the whole idea of 'the masterpiece' . . .
[It] is to Modernism what the Black Mass is to the Mass."
Nice line, that. And went on: "It is only fitting that
Duchamp's last gift to the world should be the apotheosis
of enigma, direct but infinitely mysterious . . . This
three-dimensional painting, this tableau made of pigskin,
hair, and twigs, this exercise in voyeurism, alchemy, and
self-parody, is a Declaration of Independence."

John Canaday reviewed it for the *New York Times*. He
did not sound awestruck. "This mixture of camp, high
style, prophetically opportunistic sexual exhibitionism,
surrealism, cynical wit and horseplay is pure Duchamp.
Duchamp can never be dismissed, but on the other hand
he should never be taken with total seriousness except in

the context of a concept of modern art that accepts effete exhaustion as a residual intellectual gain." He described Duchamp as "an entrancing personality who has been, along with Picasso and Matisse, one of the trio of most powerful influences on 20th century art but who, unlike his two peers, has exerted an influence primarily destructive—unless you want to say that the recognition of art as a parasitic appendage, an amusement, a vaudeville performance, is constructive in its flat admission that art has lost all connection with anything but the fluff of life . . . [F]or the first time, this cleverest of 20th-century masters looks a bit retardataire . . . A swell Duchamp it is. But a major addition to 20th century art it is not. The impression is just a bit as if we had discovered the tomb of another Pharaoh. Very interesting, but nothing new."

7 Duchamp or NOT Duchamp?

In May 1988 the SoHo artist René Moncada sent out
an invitation to join him at MoMA for the opening of
Vent-Elation. The invitation included a map to a specific
spot on the third floor of the museum between the
painting and sculpture wings, near the restrooms. His
friends must have been pleased and surprised; René had
never had work in MoMA before.

When people arrived, they found him standing
next to a gleaming aluminum ventilation grill, 12 feet
high by 2 feet wide. Citing Duchamp's principle of the
readymade—"or, in this case, the ready-installed"—he
claimed it as his art. He now had a work in the museum's
permanent collection, regardless of whether the museum
acknowledged it. Duchamp had merely thought about
declaring a building a readymade. Rene had now done it,
for at least a piece of a building.

Vent-Elation was not his only Duchampian provocation. In the late 1970s, in his SoHo art neighborhood, he
began painting a mural with giant letters declaring I AM

THE BEST ARTIST and signed it René. Later he took
to calling himself René I AM THE BEST ARTIST and
René IATBA. His arty neighbors were not pleased. Into
the 1990s the mural was repeatedly splashed with paint,
graffiti bombed, altered to say things like I AM THE
PEST FARTIST, and he kept repainting it.

He is also as enamored of the vagina as Duchamp was.
In July 1983 he dressed his friend *Screw* magazine pub-
lisher Al Goldstein as Jesus and had him carry a 5-foot
crucifix with a large, beautifully sculpted vagina on it up
the steps of St. Patrick's Cathedral. He called it *Sex and
Violence*. They were arrested on a charge of disturbing
the peace. At their trial, René argued that the cross was
a symbol of death, the vagina the source of life. Courbet
would have approved when the judge dismissed the case.

•

In 1969 the *Village Voice* called Duchamp "the most
influential artist of our time, a super-Dadaist, and a super-
intellectual, a mainspring, a wellspring, a genius. Many, if
not most, of the works we will see this coming art season
[1969–70] will be nothing more than spin-offs of his scant
but crucial oeuvre." Michael R. Taylor wrote in 2009, "If
you had said in 1968 when he died that Duchamp was as
important as Picasso, no one would have believed you.

Today it is self-evident. Duchamp was the most influential artist of the 20th century. He changed the world of art."

Tracking Duchamp's legacy in New York is not hard to do. Following his lead, artists like Moncada have strayed far from traditional definitions of what art is and how it's supposed to be made and presented. Probably no artists have taken the readymade idea farther than Mike Bidlo and Sherrie Levine. Bidlo reproduced and altered famous artists' works and claimed the results as his own in his years-long NOT series, which included NOT Picasso, NOT Pollock, NOT Warhol, NOT Man Ray— and of course NOT Duchamp, which included *Fractured Fountain*, "a porcelain urinal that Bidlo handcrafted, smashed, reassembled, and then cast into solid bronze." Levine paid similar homage with her beautiful *Fountain (Buddha)*, as well as appropriating and repurposing Edgar Degas, Brâncuși, and Walker Evans imagery.

The Fluxus movement that flourished in SoHo in the 1960s and '70s was also a direct descendant of Dada and Duchamp—or, as founder George Maciunas put it, "a fusion of Spike Jones, gags, games, Vaudeville, Cage and Duchamp." Humor, sex, audience-participation events, and a general thumbing of the nose to the stuffy art establishment characterized the group's otherwise uncategorizable work. Yoko Ono was allied with Fluxus in her SoHo years. Her ideas were profoundly influenced by

Dada and Duchamp, though, like Warhol, she hesitates to
give away too much credit. Her *Painting to Be Stepped On*
seems a manifestation of Duchamp's "use a Rembrandt
as an ironing-board." Her *Play it by Trust* is an oversized,
interactive chessboard with all-white pieces. The artist
Nam June Paik's *Zen for Film* was eight minutes of blank
screen, the film corollary of Cage's *4'33"* of silence; Paik's
wife Shigeko Kubota's 1965 *Vagina Painting* was a performance by Kubota, painting by vagina. Fluxus-adjacent
video and Internet art pioneer Douglas Davis devoted
himself to the Duchampian question of how to define art
in a post-art world.

Ray Johnson and his collaborators in the ironically
named New York Correspondence School—Johnson
preferred to spell it Correspondance, a bit of Duchampian
wordplay—took their art away from the museum and the
gallery and put it in the US mail. They sent one another
handmade postcards and small, talismanic objects that
epitomized the principle of the readymade. Johnson was
not shy about his debt to Duchamp and founded a Marcel
Duchamp Fan Club.

Some art historians have seen Cindy Sherman's
entire oeuvre of painstakingly constructed alter egos and
characters as elaborations on Rrose Sélavy.

Another way of assessing Duchamp's legacy is the
astonishingly vast and diverse literature about him. It

encompasses not only the expected artists, art scholars, and art critics, but also philosophers, scientists,
semioticians, occultists, poets, novelists, chess experts,
and at least a few crackpots. Occultists see hints of the
alchemical and the kabbalistic in his work. Those of a
more science-fictional bent believe some of his work
operates in more than three dimensions and that *Fountain*, as one scholar has put it, "referenced non-Euclidean
time-space relationships that suggested an underlying
universal esthetic." It has been noted that Duchamp and
John Dewey, the philosopher and education reformer,
were contemporaries in New York in the *Fountain* era,
and that although there's no evidence that they knew
each other, they agreed that the personal engagement of
the audience member took precedence over any esthetic
judgments handed down by experts. Building on Dewey's
approach to esthetic education, Maxine Greene started
the experimental Lincoln Center Education (LCE)
program, in Duchamp's old neighborhood, in the 1970s.

In the late 1990s scientist Stephen Jay Gould became
so fascinated with Duchamp's enigmas and paradoxes
that he and his wife Rhonda Roland Shearer founded the
nonprofit Arts Science Research Laboratory in downtown Manhattan and began the online journal *toutfait*
(*readymade* in French) to publish research and essays
exploring some of the more curious aspects of Duchamp's

oeuvre. Gould himself was especially intrigued by Duchamp's use of puns and language puzzles in the titles he gave to his works.

Asked by *Artnet* in 2025 "Does Marcel Duchamp still matter?," Ai Weiwei, who cut his teeth on the downtown Manhattan art scene, replied, "I believe Marcel Duchamp's influence remains profound—not only today but well into the future. His impact lies in how he liberated art from being purely visual, elevating it to a realm of intellect, concept, and poetic interpretation, and how he uses a new language and individual perspectives in reinterpreting reality. By individualizing art as an essential attribute of human creativity, its humanitarian essence would never disappear." Jeff Koons, whose debt to Duchamp hardly needs mentioning, said, "Duchamp is as relevant today as in his own time. Duchamp's life represents a profound belief in what we and art can become." A long list of other artists, academics, museum directors, and gallerists answered in the affirmative.

•

In August 1995, seven years after *Vent-Elation*, another amusing Duchamp-related event left MoMA's administration humiliated and speechless. A young man described in *Forbes* as "of a slightly disheveled appearance" strolled into a second-floor gallery where the museum's 1951 replica of *Bicycle Wheel* was displayed. He picked it up, threw the ungainly object over his shoulder, marched out of the museum with it, past several security guards, and got in a taxi. Sometime later he returned and tossed it over a wall into the museum sculpture garden. He was never caught. Mortified, museum administrators refused to comment.

In 2025, MoMA's permanent collection, if it can be called "permanent" after that incident, included the recovered *Bicycle Wheel*; *To Be Looked at (from the Other Side of the Glass) with One Eye, Close to, for Almost an Hour*; *3 Standard Stoppages*; *The Passage from the Virgin to the Bride*; *Anemic Cinema*; and a number of other Duchamp works. In 1973 MoMA and the Philadelphia Museum of Art cooperated on a Duchamp retrospective. In 2025 they announced they would do it again in 2026.

Anti-Duchamp art critics like Clement Greenberg and Hilton Kramer like to point out the irony in the way the anti-artist who was so against the art establishment and academies was embraced by art museums and art academics everywhere. In 1995 Kramer wrote, "the appropriation of Duchamp by the academy may be the ultimate Duchampian irony: a revolution in sensibility buried in a cemetery of scholarly footnotes."

Put another way, it may be Duchamp's ultimate victory that he persuaded a major art museum to give a permanent home to a peepshow booth, and Henry McBride's Academicians can't stop praising it and him to this day.

Further Reading

BOOKS

Bloemink, Barbara J. *The Life and Art of Florine Stettheimer.*

Brown, Milton W. *The Story of the Armory Show.*

Cabanne, Pierre. *Dialogues with Marcel Duchamp.*

Cage, John. *Silence: Lectures and Writings.*

Camfield, William A. *Duchamp: Fountain.*

Gammel, Irene. *Baroness Elsa.*

Golding, John. *Duchamp: The Bride Stripped Bare by Her Bachelors, Even.*

Guggenheim, Peggy. *Out of This Century.*

Hamilton, Richard. *The Bride Stripped Bare by Her Bachelors, Even.*

Joachimides, Christos M., and Norman Rosenthal. *The Age of Modernism: Art in the 20th Century.*

Koch, Polly (ed.). *Joseph Cornell/Marcel Duchamp . . . in resonance.*

Kostelanetz, Richard. *John Cage.*

Moncada, René. *I Am the Best Artist.*

Motherwell, Robert. *The Dada Painters and Poets.*

Naumann, Francis M. *Marcel Duchamp: The Art of Making Art in the Age of Mechanical Reproduction.*

Ray, Man. *Self Portrait*.

Roth, Moira, and Jonathan D. Katz. *Difference/Indiffer-ence: Musings on Postmodernism, Marcel Duchamp and John Cage*.

Sanouillet, Michel, and Elmer Peterson. *The Writings of Marcel Duchamp*.

Schwarz, Arturo. *The Complete Works of Marcel Duchamp*.

Taylor, Michael R. *Marcel Duchamp: Étant donnés*.

Tomkins, Calvin. *Duchamp: A Biography*.

Tomkins, Calvin. *The Bride and the Bachelors*.

Wood, Beatrice. *I Shock Myself*.

INTERNET

Duchamp Research Portal

https://www.duchamparchives.org

The International Dada Archive

https://dada.lib.uiowa.edu

toutfait

https://www.toutfait.com

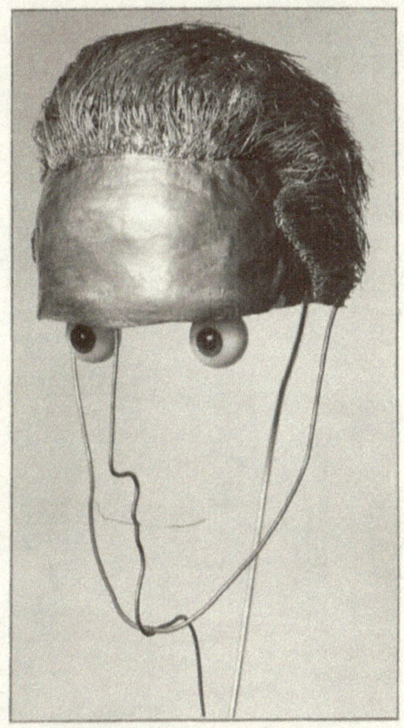

IS THIS A WORK OF ART?

Jean Crotti's "portrait of Marcel Duchamp" is perhaps the most discussed single art exhibit of the past season in New York. It is entirely constructed of wire and drawn lead—and a specially constructed pair of artificial eyes. The entire structure is supported by a single wire.

Acknowledgments

Thanks to Colin Robinson and everyone at OR Books
for making this happen. Thanks to Laura Lindgren
for her brilliant design, as well as copyediting and
typesetting. Thanks to Donald Kennison for his great
proofreading. Thanks to Francis M. Naumann for his
expert notes and corrections. Thanks to Peter-Christian
Aigner of the Gotham Center for helping us with the
launch. And thanks to Diane Ramo for reviewing drafts
and offering indispensable encouragement along the way.

About the Author

John Strausbaugh is an award-winning author, historiographer, and journalist. His most recent books include three deep explorations of New York City history. *The Village*, his epic history of Greenwich Village, was hailed as "rare and refreshing" in the *New York Times* and selected as one of *Kirkus Review*'s Best Books of 2013. *City of Sedition* (2016), his history of New York City during the Civil War, won the Fletcher Pratt Award for best nonfiction of the year, and the Eugene Feit Award in Civil War Studies. *Victory City* (2018), a paradigm-shifting look at New York during World War II, was praised as "a compulsively engaging read" (*Washington Post*) and "remarkable" (*New York Journal of Books*). His other books include *The Wrong Stuff: How the Soviet Space Program Crashed and Burned*; *Sissy Nation*; and *Rock 'Til You Drop*. He is a former editor of the downtown weekly *New York Press* and has been a contributing writer for the *New York Times*, the *Washington Post*, and other publications. He lives in Manhattan.